THE CONSULTANT'S KIT

Establishing and Operating
Your Successful Consulting Business

by

Dr. Jeffrey L. Lant

Published by JLA Publications
A Division of Jeffrey Lant Associates, Inc.
50 Follen Street, Suite 507
Cambridge, Massachusetts 02138
Tel.: 617/547-6372

Acknowledgements: As with his other books, the author has been well-served during the preparation of this volume by the time and advice of several knowledgeable individuals. He is happy to acknowledge their contributions to this study: Jim and Lucy Dube, James Duzak, Esq., and Gary Lowenstein, CPA.

The Consultant's Kit

7th printing, revised 2nd edition, October 1984

THE CONSULTANT'S KIT: TABLE OF CONTENTS

SPECIAL PREFACE FOR THE SEVENTH PRINTING!

From The Author, Dr. Jeffrey Lant

Fellow Entrepreneurs, Consultants, Independent Contractors, and Experts:

This book is a Cinderella of the book trade. Let me tell you something of its history.

After I wrote it a little over two years ago, I let a wheedling literary agent (himself, of course, a consultant) persuade me to submit a copy of the first printing, then type-written, offset printed and spiral-bound, to a publisher. Not just any publisher either but a *major* internationally-renowned house. The reader's report was ecstatic. He understood the market and recommended to his acquisitions editor that their house acquire the book.

My agent thought he had a sale, and the publisher thought he had a good mid-list book. I was tempted. After all, even though I had had two books published before, I was a novice in the business field. And the publisher was so very prestigious.

But I was nagged by a persistent doubt: if this publisher wanted the book and if I myself was sure of the market (and I was) why shouldn't I publish it myself? As the proposed sale made its way through the inevitable corporate bureaucracy, this doubt grew into a course of action. Why not indeed!

At last the formal offer arrived, by no means a whopper like *Princess Daisy,* but respectable enough. What happened next deserves a contemporary Rembrandt to do it justice: the ingénue business author throwing his oh-so-subtly persuasive agent and the big-time publisher into confusion by saying, "I think I'll keep publishing it myself."

There was a gasp of astonishment from the agent (who saw his commission evaporating) and this exchange with the editor: "You can't. You can't sell a trade paperback for $30, and you haven't got the distribution network. It'll never fly." He all but added that patronizing word, "kid."

That, ladies and gentlemen, was over 17,000 copies and a gross of over $500,000 ago. And when this printing sells out, as it undoubtedly will, that gross will be substantially over $600,000 with yet another printing on the way. Not bad for a project launched on a hunch and which a major publisher said would "never fly." Now you will understand why I treat that word "never" with a grain of salt.

Why has **THE CONSULTANT'S KIT** become the success it so evidently has?

First, it's cheap. Maybe you're one of the people who grumbled about the price of this book. Maybe you compared it to the three-pound paperback novel you recently picked up in the check-out lane at your local grocer's. Of course, they bear no comparison to each other for the cheap paperback was overpriced.

You'll be using this book in some form for the rest of your professional life, and as such the cost is frankly trifling. I know that, and I have been seriously advised to charge even more for it. It's a question, you see, of perceived value, and most people who buy this book do so enthusiastically, well understanding that they will make back its purchase cost hundreds of times. So will you — if you follow my techniques.

There's a lesson to be learned here which will influence the success of your practice: charge according to the benefit the client will get from your information. Charge, that is, according to its perceived value by the client.

You have put an enormous amount of money into becoming an expert in your field, gaining specialized information, and finding ways which will help others. Now, at a ridiculously low cost, you can begin to capitalize this investment — in often dramatic ways.

Moreover, if you're like most of the people who have bought **THE CONSULTANT'S KIT** and taken my workshop programs, you are bored, tired and frustrated with the usual 9-to-5 routine. I know I was. I hated taking orders, and I was a very bad employee. Not only did I think my bosses were often wrong about what they were doing; I had the assurance that I could do it better. This is not an attitude that most bosses like — until they hire a consultant, when they deem it essential and pay accordingly.

You have been looking for the opportunity to take your fate in hand, to use your brains and information to your own best advantage and keep for yourself a greater percentage of the benefits which you know how to deliver. Not surprisingly, while you are often frustrated on the job, you are ordinarily brimming over with creativity, a zest for life and a desire to help others. For make no mistake about it: we consultants are a very helpful lot. We like our information to be put to the best possible use solving other people's problems.

Perhaps like most of my readers and workshop participants, however, you are not an heir to great wealth. You've got the brains and the expertise but nature neglected the trust fund. In consulting that's all right. Consulting is one of the last places left where you can create a profitable business *from the first day* (as I did) with ludicrously limited capital. I can now confess that when I launched Jeffrey Lant Associates, I did so with just $100 — and no reserves in the bank. I also want to tell you that when I did I gave no thought to failure: it was a luxury I couldn't afford.

When I launched my business there was no book like **THE CONSULTANT'S KIT**, and I made as a result a panoply of mistakes. None was fatal, all were more or less wounding. Being a helpful person, I resolved to spare you the same ignominies, foolishness, and tire-spinning. So I wrote this book which is, in one way of thinking, a compilation of all my mistakes and the ways to avoid them and do things right.

For keep in mind: there are right ways and wrong ways to go about the business of being a consultant. You have to be technically expert in your field. You must spend a portion of *each* day marketing. You must promote your successes to people and organizations who want you to replicate them. You must learn how to exploit the media to become the perceived expert in your field. And you must be determined to succeed.

I remain resolutely determined, and I advise you to take on the same insistent attitude about your own success. Not everyone will like you for it. Most people are slothful, disorganized and prone to associating with others who share these lackluster traits. Not successful consultants, however. It's another luxury we can't afford.

As my colleagues know, I live, eat, sleep and breathe my business. If for Henry Kissinger (now, of course, a consultant himself), power is the ultimate aphrodisiac, then for me it's making a sweet deal, a very tangible accomplishment. I delight in finding new ways of working smart: cutting my hours while reaping ever greater profits on projects that make use of more and still more of my talents. As you master the techniques of **THE CONSULTANT'S KIT**, you will come to work as efficiently.

What is clear is that consulting demands your creativity. I have never, never in my life been more consistently creative than since I launched my consulting practice. It demands your commitment, your drive, your energy, your constant enthusiasm. Continually. But consulting repays this investment in two very important ways.

At one of my jobs, my employer in a burst of candor told me that she ''owned'' me, and she demonstrated her power by calling and demanding my attention and presence whenever the whim took her. Most bosses feel they own their employees whether or not they are as starkly open about it as my former employer. Now, however, I am independent and my time is literally my own. Going into consulting was my Emancipation Proclamation.

Equally importantly, consulting is a way to do well while doing good. When I established my consulting practice I had a minimal net worth. Now I am nationally known and a Pillar of the Community.

Thus consulting has freed me from the often abasing business of working for anyone — ever again. It has provided me with a world of travel opportunities — all on someone else's money. It has given me continuing national media exposure. And, always, the satisfaction of helping others.

No wonder I am so enthusiastic about the profession and continually urging it on those who have the potential to succeed as a consultant. Unfortunately, not everyone has this potential, a regretable fact but true.

If you are comfortable taking orders from someone else, stay where you are. You're in the right place.

If you can't handle the anxiety that comes from losing a regular paycheck, stay where you are — and for the sake of your job security, stop griping.

If you don't feel comfortable dealing with decision makers as a peer, stay where you are. Consultants, like cream, rise to the top.

If you need to exercise power regularly, need to have people jump to do your bidding, stay where you are. Consultants are influential rather than powerful. We work through others. We are experts at persuasion and communication. Simon Legree, please note, was not a consultant.

If you like nice tight hours and a regular way of doing business, stay where you are. Trouble keeps no hours and consultants are notorious for their long work hours and ability to handle many disparate projects simultaneously.

But enough of the negatives. You didn't buy this book to be told to stay away from consulting, although that's an added service I gratefully provide. You bought it to become the consulting success you deserve to be.

This being the case, let me, as your consultant, give you a little more advice. Follow this book conscientiously. I know that these methods work, and I recommend them to you. Follow, too, the recommended publicity, promotion, public relations and media access techniques in my book **THE UNABASHED SELF-PROMOTER'S GUIDE.** Paid advertising *is* useful. I certainly don't disdain it, but I have built my reputation, raised my fees and collared clients (probably including you) from my ability to generate generous amounts of free media attention. You should do the same. As with this book, the price of **THE UNABASHED SELF-PROMOTER'S GUIDE** is miniscule compared to the lifetime of benefits you will reap from faithfully following its advice.

In conclusion, I take this opportunity to thank my readers, all of whom I consider my friends. For you are that and more. I consider that you — like me — are the cutting edge of change in this country. For you have technical information of unparalleled usefulness, apt solutions to vexing problems, and the kind of dogged determination and conviction that built the nation.

Here's to us, then, the best and the brightest, scouts into the future. And here's to **THE CONSULTANT'S KIT,** our map non pareil!

As in the past, I know you will continue to be in touch with me. I know that you will send me your good ideas, your tested techniques and will continue to teach me, the teacher.

I salute you — and I thank you!

J.L.
Cambridge, Massachusetts
May, 1984

CHAPTER 1

THE CONSULTANT'S WORLD: IS IT FOR YOU?

Is any one of these your situation?

- For years, you have been working at a 9-to-5 office job that makes little use of the investment you made in a college or graduate school. Despite long hours and hard work, you barely make enough money to keep pace with inflation. You are frustrated, bored, and angry with your boss, and with the hierarchy and politics of the office, all of which squelch your creativity and ignore your ideas. You have little power, influence, or access to decision makers, and you are tired of placating authority, which may not be any more knowledgable than you. The future appears bleak. Suspecting that creativity, talent, intelligence, and drive are incompatible with your working for your employer, you begin to think that, given the chance, you could have a fast-paced, stimulating, growing career.

- Your work as a teacher or social worker is exhausting, rather than exhilarating, and is burning you out. There is little opportunity to advance or to earn more, despite your excellent performance. You're powerless, unappreciated, and frustrated because problems abound that you cannot solve, even if you know the solution.

- You are a college professor who discovers that colleagues are augmenting their salaries by marketing their expertise outside the university. You find that your research has tremendous market potential, and someone else is reaping the benefit of your ideas. Professional journals, clamoring for your articles, underpay you. You believe your knowledge could be a source of income if you knew how to project yourself beyond the academic environment.

- Retirement is approaching, and you would like to work only a few days a week. Yet you don't want to spend the rest of your life on the golf course or in an easy chair. You've developed marketable skills over the years, and they shouldn't be wasted.

- After several years of working, you took time out to build a family. Now, the children are starting school and you want to reenter the work force. Yet, you want to be home for your children when they need you.

- You're close to finishing business school. Starting your own business is your dream, and it seems more attractive than working for someone else.

- You are a consultant, but can't seem to get ahead. You've been marketing your service locally and would like to establish yourself on a nationwide basis.

If one of these descriptions—or a dozen others like them—fits you, consider consulting. If you are reading this book, you must already be seriously considering consulting, but you may not know how to go about it, or you may not be sure that it is for you.

This book is designed to provide you with the general skills needed by a consultant, regardless of his field or level of expertise, and this chapter will help you decide whether consulting will suit you. This is a "how-to" book that tells you how to market, negotiate, write contracts, set up a network, set up shop, find more information, and establish yourself as a leader in your field.

What Is a Consultant?

You probably hear a lot about consultants, but you may have only a vague idea of what a consultant does. Some reasons for this are that the use of consultants is growing rapidly, and they are used in increasingly varied ways.

Certain characteristics typify consulting, however. First, a consultant has developed an acknowledged expertise in a specific area. Consultants typically operate outside an organization's hierarchy. As a result, their power is usually advisory rather than direct. A consultant is not a regular employee. He is contracted on a formal or informal basis to do a long- or short-term task. He is paid on a project, per diem, or retainer basis and does not receive paid vacations, insurance, social security, or other benefits. A consultant is generally a self-employed, independent agent, or a small, self-contained "service business." Some consultants are employed by a consulting group independently of an organization or as a division of the organization for which they work. The techniques in this book will be helpful to all consultants but especially to independent practitioners.

There is a fine line between consulting for an organization and free-lancing for it. Primarily, a consultant advises, and a free-lancer acts. For example, a free-lance computer programmer may be hired to create a program according to predetermined operational needs. A computer consultant, however, would analyze a company's needs and determine how a program can improve business operations. There is a difference in the level of expertise between a free-lancer and a consultant. A person who has few years of experience may begin as a free-lancer. But, because free-lancers are frequently exposed to situations in which their skills can be used, they quickly acquire the experience needed to be an adviser or a consultant.

A Brief History of Consulting

In the 1950s, consulting was the norm in only a few fields, including law, accounting, personnel recruitment, and technical areas. During the '60s, some professional consultants, especially accountants, such as Arthur Young Associates and Booz and Allen, began to organize. At the same time, "brain banks" began to proliferate, and began to work on government contracts and to draw on universities for ideas.

The 1960s also brought a tremendous surge in science and technology, causing a dual impact on consulting. First, many industries found it more cost-effective to buy research rather than to invest in permanent research facilities because it enabled them to use experts and specialists without making a permanent commitment. As the new technologies filtered into business and industry, specialists were needed to advise on use and application—a pattern that is now well-established. When new technologies are introduced, industry becomes more complex, and duties become more specialized. As a result, a class of consultants will spring up to fill these new needs.

Another factor in the U.S. during the '50s and '60s was a gradual shift from a production-oriented economy to a service-oriented economy. Consulting is a service and, as such, fits neatly into this trend.

The 1970s brought several new developments that further contributed to the growth and acceptance of consulting. During the economic recession, businesses began to trim operating costs. It made more sense to hire consultants as needed rather than to maintain a large staff. At the same time, growing specialization, greater complexity in management, and an increase of regulations demanded highly refined expertise. Consulting firms grew, large businesses established internal consulting groups, and individual practices proliferated.

The latest evolution in consulting is a loosely knit association of experts from various fields. This usually begins with a consultant offering a service and discovering that he has too much business to handle alone or that his client needs some services that the consultant cannot offer. Rather than forfeit a client, the consultant hires other consultants, called associates.

Associates may be people with regular jobs who are interested only in an occasional assignment, or they may be independent consultants. The principal consultant may act primarily as an agent who organizes teams to fulfill certain needs. The members of the team may become familiar with each other and negotiate contracts with each other to fill their clients' needs. Although these relationships can be complex, confusing, and competitive, they also have some advantages. For example, a team can handle projects that an individual can't, and can create unique combinations of skills. A team can also form and dissolve itself when needed.

This concept is strongly related to the "supermarket-of-services" approach; in which a consultant who specializes in a particular field recognizes that his clients regularly require a range of easily definable services. For example, the clients of a small business administration consultant may need regular help in publicity, theft control, bookkeeping, accounting, and other services in which the consultant lacks expertise. The principal consultant then identifies other consultants who can provide these services, offers package arrangements to clients, and sub-contracts to other consultants. Or, he may refer the other consultants to the clients in return for a commission or percentage of the fee.

Consultants—the new breed of entrepreneurs—are now in every field. Dun and Bradstreet lists about 100 sub-specialties in business management alone in which a consultant might specialize. *Money* magazine conservatively estimates business-management consulting to be a $2-billion business employing about 50,000 people. Business is only one sector of the economy that uses consultants. They also are widely used in education, nonprofit organizations, government, hospital administration, publishing, advertising, entertainment, and personnel services. There are consultants for party planning, interior design, family finances, personal image, and career growth. There are even consultants who will organize homes and offices or advise on running garage sales.

Such consultants start because there is a market for almost every type of skill. The only limitation in consulting is a person's imagination. No matter how obvious the solutions to problems might seem, people can use help in solving them, and they are willing to pay for that help.

Why Do Organizations Hire Consultants?

Organizations or individuals typically hire consultants when they cannot do a job themselves or when it is not in their best interests to do it themselves. The most common reasons that consultants are hired include:

- To augment a staff: A business can save a tremendous amount of money by hiring consultants as needed because, although consultants often receive high fees, it is more expensive for the business to maintain a consultant in-house, paying both salary and an additional thirty percent in benefits. This is particularly true when a task needs to be

4

performed only occasionally, which is the case with a seasonal or contract-oriented business. In some cases, especially in creative fields, hiring outside consultants is a way to acquire new talent on a regular basis.

- To provide expertise: A company may hire a consultant who has a demonstrated track record in a specific area and exposure to a wide variety of situations.

- To provide objectivity: A consultant can provide a fresh, impartial viewpoint. A consultant may get suggestions implemented that someone inside the company could not. One reason for this is that a consultant does not have a vested interest in any one plan. The consultant is free to give advice without having his personal or political motivations questioned.

- To identify problems: Insiders are often not objective enough to identify a problem and its symptoms.

- To act as a catalyst: Consultants know how to initiate change. They can overcome the inertia typically found in structured organizations. For example, a consultant can communicate with personnel at all levels of an organization's hierarchy and, when necessary, facilitate communications among employees at different hierarchical levels.

- To instruct: A consultant may teach his skills to a client and teach employees how to apply new technologies or how to operate in a changing organizational structure.

- To act as political hatchetmen. Consultants are often asked to do work that nobody else wants to do, such as firing top management or eliminating divisions in a company. There are various other political reasons why a consultant might be hired. For example, if an organization needs major changes that will not be well-received, a consultant can implement them and disappear.

- To influence others: Some consultants are hired because they have access to influential people. For example, a consultant who has participated in government can connect his client with a government contractor. This practice is most prevalent in the public sector, but it also occurs in business and industry. Any large business that contracts work may hire power brokers.

- To oversee multi-business operations: When two or more businesses negotiate a contract on a project, a consultant may be brought in to oversee the operations. This is most likely when a high financial risk is involved. For example, a bank that is providing a mortgage to a complex real-estate development may hire a consultant to oversee the developer and the general contractor.

Attitudes Toward Consultants

Organizations and individuals often seem to have a love/hate relationship with consultants. On one hand, consultants suggest infallibility; they are a guiding light glimpsed in an organization's moment of despair. They may be an organization's last hope.

But there are also many negative feelings toward consultants. For example, there is a saying about a consultant who borrows your watch to tell you the time and then walks off with the watch. Some consultants don't perform their jobs well, and once a client has had a bad experience, he can't easily forget it. Some reasons for distrust, however, can be attributed to a consultant's role and to a client's errors. Some of the main reasons a client may hesitate in hiring a consultant include:

- Conflicts of interest: Late in 1980, the television show "60 Minutes" aired a segment on "Beltway Bandits," the large consulting firms ringing Washington, D.C. The exposé focused on auditing firms simultaneously consulting for the Department of Energy, large oil companies, and OPEC nations. Such conflicts of interest can occur in any consulting firm. In many cases, it is better in the long run to choose clients carefully and to avoid conflicts of interest in advance rather than incur a client's distrust.

- Large fees: A successful engagement with a consultant can yield high returns for a client, but clients often resent the consultant's high fees.

- Client misunderstanding: Clients often don't know how to use consultants or don't know what a consultant can do. A client may expect a consultant to solve problems, rather than to guide the clients on how to solve problems. If this is not clear when an engagement begins, disastrous results may follow for both parties.

- Ill-defined problems: Hiring a consultant may fail when the client's problems have not been properly defined. A client may direct the consultant to a symptom rather than to a true problem. Or, the client may not acknowledge a problem's true cause, even after the consultant has defined it. These causes for failure may originate with the client, but it is the consultant's responsibility to analyze properly and to clarify the situation. Consultants may also be guilty of misdirecting their energies, which is particularly true when consultants develop narrow perspectives and ignore factors outside their areas of expertise. For example, a specialist in financing may not recognize that funds are being wasted on an inappropriate technology being used in the productions department. Or, a consultant may insist on zero-based-budgeting when it is totally inappropriate to a firm's problem.

- Poorly packaged solutions: Another typical situation is one in which consultants offer valid recommendations but fail to get them implemented. The reason is that a

6

consultant is not responsive to a client's character or situation. For example, the J.P. Jones Company has always operated under the autocratic rule of Mr. Jones. A progressive management specialist enters the picture and advises the adoption of a team-management approach. The suggestion may be good, but Jones and his top officers are not likely to accept or to implement it.

- Staff resentment: Top management sometimes uses consultants as spies and hatchetmen, causing unrest and distrust among the rest of the staff. Employees will probably resent having a consultant hired over them and paid a tremendous fee. Meanwhile, the employees are required to perform their daily routines on the authority of an intruder. Furthermore, the consultant does not have to follow his own suggested course of action, which exacerbates the situation. As a British prime minister said in a different context, "Consultants have the prerogative of the harlot throughout the ages: influence without responsibility."

- Lack of professional codes: A client has no guarantee on a consultant's ethics or proficiency. Although a few professional associations are trying to establish codes and certification procedures, the client typically can only hope that a consultant will be honest.

- Prejudice: Top management is predominantly "old-school," and old prejudices die hard. Consultants who are women or members of minority groups will probably encounter prejudice in their dealings with clients.

These errors could leave the client with a very poor opinion of the consultant and in even worse straits than before hiring the consultant. However, common sense and ethical performance can overcome many of these problems. It helps to know in advance why he is being hired and what negative attitudes toward consultants the client already has. As consultants are used more and more frequently to maintain an organization's health and promote its growth rather than to save it from the brink of disaster, the positive aspects of consulting will outshadow the negative ones. The consistent growth of consulting indicates that a positive attitude is prevailing.

Should You be a Consultant?

Switching from the 9-to-5 world to the consultant's world could be one of the greatest changes you will make. It could have as great an impact on your life as entering the work force, getting married, or moving to a new locale. Some people find it liberating, but others find it to be in conflict with their personalities, lifestyles, and work styles. Before embarking on this route, seriously consider how consulting will suit you.

From the day you begin school, your life is ruled by clocks, bells, schedules, and authority figures. To suddenly find yourself free of this structure can be disconcerting, even if you have always resented that structure. For the first time, you are responsible for your every action. An independent, self-disciplined person will probably make this adjustment within six to 12 months. It is possible to develop these characteristics, but anyone who has always punched a time clock without considering it an indignity probably should not consider a career in consulting.

Consultants view the use of time quite differently than do most workers, perhaps because there is such a direct relationship between how much consultants do and how much they earn. Just when you have everything scheduled and in place, an important contract with a tight deadline appears. When you're just getting started you may not be free to deny a request because you need the money and the client. As a result, you stretch your workday a few extra hours and stretch your week to six or seven days. Just as unexpectedly, you may find yourself with an afternoon off in the middle of the week, resulting in a pleasant feeling of guilt. If you were employed by another person you would have at least to appear to be working. Now, you have nobody for whom to perform . Eventually, you will learn to pace yourself and your marketing and to sub-contract some work to keep your clients and your peace of mind. However, consultants are usually troubleshooters , and trouble does not keep regular hours. As a result, life will never be as orderly as it was when you worked a 9-to-5 job. Consulting changes your lifestyle in many ways. The line between work and private life disappears, particularly for consultants working at home. Depending on your field and market, traveling will probably increase. You will not see one set of people on a daily basis, and you become acutely aware that a regular check is not guaranteed. For some, the constant change is disorienting. Integrating personal life and professional life may impinge on your family. And the financial insecurity can be nerve-racking.

Enter consulting with the expectation of a six-month dry period and build a nest egg before quitting your job. Even if you are fortunate enough to be signing contracts on your first day, the payment checks might not appear for months. It typically takes two to four years to build a clientele and reputation that will provide financial security. A consultant may be offered regular jobs by clients. And when bills seem insurmountable, you may be tempted to accept one of those offers, but resist. The only part of the routine life you really want is the pay check. The attractions of consulting are the ones that will serve you well as a consultant, but will make you an unhappy, frustrated employee.

What are those attractions? Assuming you like your work to begin with, consulting is a constant professional challenge. No more snail-paced growth will occur. Instead, your career develops in leaps and bounds. Each new client brings a new problem. A good consultant will search for the solution that best suits the circumstances. Mental agility should take a quantum leap. Be highly analytical and able to size up situations quickly. Most importantly, you must not have a "pigeon-hole" mentality, but must be open to widely varying situations. You must be able to gather information from disparate soures to create new solutions.

Consulting also demands excellent communication and social skills. Dealing with top management on an equal basis for the first time can be difficult. A consultant must candidly, civilly ask probing questions of authorities. You will probably move through the rank and file of an organization and must present yourself self-confidently. You must also be sensitive and receptive, be able to analyze people quickly, without appearing to do so. This requires good listening skills. A consultant must also be able to teach without being condescending.

Most of a consultant's marketing strategy will rely heavily on these skills. You must believe in yourself personally and professionally and must convey that feeling to others. You must believe that your services are crucial to your clients; otherwise people would not pay for those services. If you feel uncomfortable telephoning a stranger or can't tell a chief executive officer who is 30 years your senior, "I can help you," you are not a good consulting candidate.

Many consultants initially feel uncomfortable selling themselves. One reason for failure is that novices spend too much time honing profesional skills rather than marketing themselves. You must be willing to package yourself, to convey an image of skill, savoir-faire, strength and knowledgeability from the start.

You must dress the part. Neither blue jeans nor plaid polyester inspire confidence in a board of directors. You must also be willing to sell yourself constantly — at parties, to acquaintances, and to friends. You will eventually stop feeling awkward about this, but you cannot avoid it.

In addition to all the social skills, a consultant must be able to write well and to type. Although you can hire a typist, it may cramp your style, schedule and budget because a large volume of paper communications is needed. Good administrative and organizational skills, from plotting a marketing strategy to filing, are also needed. If you lack these skills, take a course in them.

A consultant's life is fast-paced. Consulting is more than a job; it is a tremendously exciting challenge. If you thrive on pressure, love adventure, like helping people, and are outgoing and confident, you will like consulting. If you have some, but not all, of these characteristics, give the decision serious thought. It is possible to develop these characteristics, but if this lifestyle seems too demanding and foreign, try another career.

CHAPTER II

DEFINING A SPECIALTY

While some people enter consulting with a clear concept of the services they intend to offer and a market for those services, most embark on this enterprise with only a vague notion of their skills. The exercises in this chapter will help you to explore your full potential, select those skills you wish to develop, and determine the state of the market.

Exercise 1: Skills and Attributes

You have probably never made a full accounting of your skills and attributes. There is rarely an opportunity to list every ability and characteristic you have developed. Perhaps you consider this superfluous, but it is not.

The exercises in this chapter are based on techniques commonly used by career counselors. You will not only embark on a new career, but will job-hunt. These exercises are relevant for several reasons. First, people typically grossly underestimate their ability. A computer specialist may be totally unaware of having developed sophisticated communications skills while soliciting information from users regarding programming needs. Housewives fail to acknowledge their ability to budget finances or to manage tasks. Teachers may not realize they have been negotiating with students. Typists may not realize they are good writers. If you don't recognize your skills, you cannot present them to a client.

Second, as you refine this list, evaluate your skills. You might find, for example, that you can compose a letter with only one draft or plan a reception for 25 people in an afternoon.

After this process, you will know if you can perform a service when a client asks, how long it will take you, and how much you should charge.

Third, if a client questions your ability to perform a task, you will be able to respond, saying "I can interview 10 staff members in one day because I know how to prepare a questionnaire. I also have excellent communications skills, a great deal of stamina, and a remarkable memory."

The comment of a psychologist I met at a meeting provides an idea of how significant this process can be in terms of recognizing abilities. She said that if she were asked to manage a coal mine, she could do so, even though she had never seen a coal mine in her life. Why? Because she knew she had the ability to gather information, to make an intelligent decision on the basis of that information, to get other people to cooperate by providing information. In other words, she not only had the necessary management skills, but she knew she had those skills.

Finally, if you have been fired from your job, or have quit because you were about to be fired, you have probably had your confidence undermined. An honest, personal assessment of your skills and attributes will help reorient you, get you back on your feet, and make you aware of where you stand.

This brings us to **Rule 1** of this exercise: This list is for you. You must explore your personality and be candid about your evaluation.

Rule 2: Divide your list into two sections—skills and attributes. Skills are developed or acquired abilities, such as researching, writing, typing, or computer programming. Attributes are inherent characteristics, such as intelligence, attractiveness, or an analytical mind.

Rule 3: List everything. You may fill 15 or 20 pages. Include such skills as sewing, cooking, filing, speed-reading, and interviewing. The same is true of attributes. Nice hair, good posture, or a well-modulated voice are as important as a good memory or the ability to learn a foreign language quickly.

Rule 4: Be specific. If you write, "I have good communications skills," use that as a topic heading and note details below it: "I can speak in front of a large audience, using a microphone, with no advance warning," or "I can facilitate discussions among several distrustful executives." Note how well you perform a task and how much time it takes you.

Rule 5: The list is on-going and needs constant updating, reviewing, refining, and additions.

Some categories to consider, along with some examples of particular skills and attributes, are included in this sample list.

Attributes

Educational/Intellectual

These are things I can do:
- perform statistical analyses commonly used in psychology
- perform lab experiments with animals
- create questionnaires
- use most standard psychology and sociology computer programs
- read German fluently
- read and speak French fluently
- project staff needs on basis of anticipated production growth

These are characteristics I possess:
- an analytical mind
- an intuitive understanding of what motivates workers
- an inquiring mind, especially about my field
- the ability to generalize from specifics
- a willingness to keep pace with developments in my field

Communications

- write moderately well
- prepare a report in only three drafts
- create audiovisual presentations
- use an extensive vocabulary
- the ability to project my voice well
- confidence before a crowd
- the ability to elicit personal comments and feelings regarding jobs
- the ability to relate to people at all levels of an organization's hierarchy

Office Abilities

- type 35 words per minute
- file, including cross-indexing
- bookkeeping
- the ability to maintain order
- the ability to create systems
- a facility with numbers

- dismantle and assemble a car
- repair most appliances
- use and repair audiovisual equipment
- carve
- paint interiors
- ability to work with electric and mechanical equipment
- steady hands
- a good eye for measurements
- excellent dexterity

Some other categories you might include are management, administration, personality, sociability, arts, finances, and sports.

If you get stuck, your daily routine should suggest the skills and attributes that you use. For example, if you plan a luncheon meeting for a half-dozen associates, you must analyze their personalities to ensure that no extreme conflicts will arise. You must also negotiate to settle on a time and place for the meeting, plan an agenda, and present your own ideas.

Exercise 2: Differentiate Abilities

The next step is to divide the items on the list into two categories: those that pertain to your specialty and those that will be helful to you as a consultant. Some items will overlap. For example, one of my technical specialties is advising nonprofit organizations on raising money. Some of the skills related to this include identifying funding resources, writing letters soliciting help, writing proposals, developing a board of directors, and researching. Skills and attributes that are helpful to me as a consultant include: dressing well, maintaining a good phone manner, being courteous and prompt, typing, and drawing up contracts. Some of these items apply to both categories. Researching, for example, is essential both to being a consultant and to being a fund-raising specialist.

If this exercise is to be helpful, an exhaustive, honest, personal inventory is essential. If you experience this be assured of recognizing your marketable skills.

Exercise 3: Skills and Attributes That Are Lacking

Few people can assess the skills and attributes they have, and they assiduously avoid evaluating their liabilities. Such an evaluation is neither easy nor pleasant, but this is, once again, a good time for an honest, personal, and exhaustive appraisal of your shortcomings. List both the skills or attributes that you lack and those you can improve. Be specific. For example, if you bite your nails or bite them only during important meetings, list that. You may want to refer to the assets list and consider any gaps. For example, if the category for communications skills was sparsely furnished in the first exercise, it will be extensive in the liabilities list. If you get stuck, use the same procedure as before. Your daily routine should suggest help for any difficulties you encounter. If the thought of calculating per-ounce costs in the supermarket seems like more trouble than its worth, list "math" or "mental arithmetic" as a deficiency. A graphic designer may ask, "Why do I need arithmetic?" Well, consider what happens when you must give a client an on-the-spot estimate of costs for materials or for your fee.

The purpose of this exercise is to help you identify those technical skills or personal attributes that you must develop. You may decide, on the basis of the results of this exercise, to take a writing course or hire a speech coach.

On the other hand, you may decide that you do not want to change. You might decide that biting your nails is irrelevant to being a photographer, and if your client sees it as an indication of nervousness or an artistic temperament, that's too bad. You may find that although you can't eliminate your liabilities, you can avoid them.

As with the first exercise, this is an on-going process. You cannot correct everything at once; prioritize. Decide which skills or attributes are most essential to your success as a consultant and work on those first. Difficulty with communications should be your top priority. As you progress in your career, you may identify new needs. For example, you may be making a good living as an interior designer for homes and then realize that top fees are paid to office designers. You should then study offices, collect catalogs of office furniture, and perhaps take a course at a design school. Developing your expertise will be discussed later in this chapter. But first, another exercise.

Exercise 4: The Ideal Project

Write an inventory of every project you want. This is a fantasy list; allow your imagination and ambition to roam. If you teach art history and would like to become an art-investment consultant to the chief executives of Fortune 500 companies, that is a valid entry for this inventory. If you are a housewife who majored in home economics 15 years ago and now want to consult to a major university on the nutritional needs of young adults, list that.

This will probably be your shortest list, especially at the beginning. If you have only a vague idea about consulting, you most likely are not aware of the full range of potential projects, but don't get discouraged. Your list will grow quickly.

Exercise 5: Identify Opportunities

This is the first step in making the "projects" list grow. Catalog other people's needs. There is no organization in the world that couldn't function better. If you don't believe that, look closely at the organization that you work for or one that you have worked for. Every complaint that you or your co-workers have indicates that the organization needs something. List those needs.

Over the course of several days, note every identified problem. For example, if you observe a handicapped person who is having difficulty entering a building, providing an access for the handicapped is a potential project. In a restaurant, you notice the plants are withered or dry and find that caring for plants in public places is a need (and a rapidly developing service). While passing a hospital, you notice an ill woman who is trying to cope with her two children and wonder who will take care of the children while she sees the doctor. You have thus identified a need for child care services in medical facilities. Add these to the list.

The purpose of this exercise is to help you internalize the process of problem identification. Consultants are always selling themselves, not in relation to jobs but in relation to problems for which they may have solutions. You must pay attention to problem situations: another person's problem is an opportunity. If you think as a consultant does, you will not perceive problems as irritations but as potential projects. Some problems are the responsibility of an organization, a department, or a person in an organization. You may wish to offer your services to that party.

Some problems will relate to your area of expertise more than others. So, disregard those you can do nothing about. Your list will help you to focus on the services that are needed and which ones you can offer.

Exercise 6: Closing the Gap

You have probably begun to recognize that there is a gap between what you are equipped to do and what you would like to do. It would be impossible for one book to teach every consultant everything he needs to know about a particular specialty, or even about consulting. But there are myriad resources available, and this exercise, one that you will probably continue indefinitely, is essentially a guide to exploring and using resources. Throughout this quest, you should collect and catalog all materials, get your name on as many pertinent mailing lists as possible, and ferret out all the good ideas you encounter. Unless an idea is owned by copyright or patent, don't hesitate to make it your own.

1. Bibliography: The bibliography in the back of this book is unusual. I have searched several libraries for the available literature on consulting. There are relatively few books on general consulting, but many are concerned with specific areas of consulting, such as accounting or consulting to small businesses and can be useful to any consultant. References to related skills, such as writing for business or negotiating, are also included.

2. Periodicals: There are several magazines and newsletters of value to small businesses. *Inc., Entrepreneur,* and *Venture* are among the better ones. Consider subscribing to one of these and/or to the *Wall Street Journal.*

There are thousands of popular and trade magazines published in this country. Track down those relating to your specialty. If your library has a limited collection, get a periodical directory and send for sample copies. Subscribe to and read the relevant ones regularly. You should know as much as possible about your field. Newsletters are more difficult to find, and their quality varies. The National Newsletter Association, which has regional branches, may help to locate worthwhile publications.

3. Government agencies and publications. The federal government is one of the largest service organizations and publishers. If someone wants to be an environmental consultant, he should know what the Environmental Protection Agency is doing. Sociologists should keep an eye on the Department of Health and Human Services. If pursued with persistence, government agencies can yield valuable resources for almost every field. Those working in highly technical fields should consider subscribing to the National Technical Information Service. Its reports and services are sometimes expensive, but its bibliographies include every report paid for by the federal government.

Several more general agencies may also be of help. The Internal Revenue Service, for example, offers regular workshops in major cities, in bookkeeping and tax preparation. A listing of some of their relevant publications is included in the bibliography. The Small Business Administration, via the Service Corps of Retired Executives, also offers workshops and advice on establishing businesses and solving problems. While SCORE tends to be retail- and manufacturing-oriented, its representatives may be able to help. They also publish several pamphlets, some of which are listed in the bibliography.

The Department of Labor, Bureau of Labor Statistics, compiles information on wages in specific fields, broken down by region. DOL also prepares forecasts on specific occupations.

4. Universities and schools: When you have identified some of your educational needs, you will probably seek out universities and public school systems, some of which offer continuing education courses. Public-school courses are usually less expensive and less sophisticated than college courses. A curriculum will help you decide. Or you may decide that you don't need an instructor; what you have read is sufficient. You may be able to avoid a university's high tuition by auditing a course. If you take a course, use the instructor as a resource and establish a relationship with him if possible. Many instructors or professors are pleased to find an astute, inquisitive student and will eagerly share their knowledge. They may be the best free source of information. Professionals with an equal amount of knowledge put a price tag on advice. You may even choose a course on the basis of who is teaching rather than what is being taught.

5. Professional and related associations. There is an association for almost every imaginable profession. These associations range from well-known, powerful groups, such as the American Medical Association or bar associations to such localized sects as the Boston Boot and Shoe Club. There may well be several competing groups in one field. These associations can provide useful, detailed information on what is happening in your field and on who is important. One of the greatest services associations may offer is a list of your competitors. Gather all the data you can and attend meetings and seminars. This could be the best tool for analyzing the market. A few large consulting associations are listed in the bibliography.

Related associations may also provide useful information. For example, the Massachusetts Cultural Alliance, Boston, offers regular workshops on bookkeeping and copyright laws for artists.

6. Civic and fraternal associations: To locate a local expert in your field, investigate such groups as the Rotary Club, the Kiwanis, or the Knights of Columbus, which often maintain directories of members' occupations.

18

7. Consultants: Unless you live in a major city or university town, you may never have met a consultant. If you have used the resources discussed above, you should know several. Arrange a meeting with a successful consultant in your own field or in a strongly related one. Expect to pay for his time and regard this session as a regular consulting relationship. To a consultant, time is money. To avoid wasting money, be well-prepared for the meeting. Write questions in advance. You may have to probe for answers and pull the interview back on course to gear the questions to the specific answers needed. If the responses are too general or a repeat of information you already have, ask for more detailed information. Find out what services he provides, to whom, and at what price. If he has a mailing, press, or client list, have your name added to it.

8. Leaders: Identify the leaders in your field and learn from them. They most likely have published books or articles and may offer workshops or presentations. They are your primary competitors, and you will hear their names from your clients. You must know what they do, how they present themselves, what their specialty is, and how much they charge. When you offer your services to a client, they may say, "Isn't that what Mr. Leader does?" You can answer, "No, he does something else. This is my specialty." Or, "Yes, but he charges three times as much as I do." You may even adjust your line of service so you will not be in direct competition with a well-established leader.

Exercise 7: Defining a Service Line

The preceding exercises have all been preparing you to define your service line. By now, you should have a fairly clear conception of what you can do and want to do. This exercise is to list your services.

As with the previous lists, be very specific. "Communications consulting" is a general heading. "Prepare a business executive for a press conference" is more specific. Many novices will hesitate to be so specific and will want to keep their service line broad for fear of turning away business or of developing in a way that differs from their ultimate goals. But just because you cannot offer services now that you can offer in the future does not mean that you shouldn't list your current services. Your services will develop, shift, and be refined. It's part of being a consultant.

When I printed my first brochure, I was surprised when an associate told me that my presentation and service line would change within a year. His prophecy proved true: I had outgrown what the brochure described because I learned from the experience of being in business and changed the services that I offered.

There is also a temptation when starting a business to accept any project even if it is not your line of interest. In developing your service line, you should not take assignments under some circumstances. For example, if a client is hiring you as a spy and you do not want to risk your reputation, you must not take the job. This is difficult if you were fired from your previous job or are suffering from low self-esteem. Accepting an engagement out of fear that nothing better will be offered will undermine your self-esteem even further.

It is not advisable to take on every job that is offered because it diverts you from becoming an acknowledged expert in your field. You cannot be expert at everything; if you try, you will burn out—a serious problem for consultants. Maintain an upbeat air, and simultaneously maintain long, irregular hours. Trying everything new prevents you from developing routines. Routinizing a task or a procedure can lower its strain. It's much like learning a dance step or a sport, such as tennis. You concentrate on getting your hands and feet in the right place at the right time. Not until you know the right steps and moves can you become good. It is better to become progressively more expert in a specific area. This will make the job and your marketing easier, and will increase your pay. Research indicates that even the largest consulting firms are emphasizing specialization because it is more marketable and profitable.

Another common misconception is that your service must be unique. Recognized expertise is more important than uniqueness, but talent alone is not enough. Someone with talent must use any opportunity to refine and develop that talent. For example, a talented school teacher who knows that large budget cuts will soon put many teachers out of jobs cannot count on his talent to save him. He must identify the problem, offer solutions, and choose a solution that will be to his benefit.

When you do have a truly unique service, indicate its uniqueness to your potential clients. Explain your service and how it will help solve the client's problems. For example, if you list your service as preparing executives for press conferences, clarify this by showing how you do it: "I use staff brain-storming sessions to anticipate questions from the press, which will be trying to sensationalize any news. The chief executive must be prepared to respond to hostile or irrelevant questions."

Finally, one common reason that consultants fail is that they try to start at the top and learn everything before they begin consulting. If you want to work for Fortune 500 companies you should aim for that goal, but start with what you can do now. Use the corner grocery store or the neighborhood dance school as your testing ground. While working these accounts, build your skills, learn how to keep an engagement running smoothly, develop your reputation, and improve your marketing techniques.

CHAPTER III

YOU CAN'T SUCCEED WITHOUT A CONTACT NETWORK

"Networking" is one of those words now being bandied about, yet the concept is old. The country's top business executives and professionals have always relied on the "old-boy network" to accomplish their goals. More recently, women trying to enter the world of business or politics realized they needed their own networks to succeed, and, in trying to figure out the rules of the game, have generated a plethora of books and articles on the subject.

As a consultant, you must develop a contact network. It is the most essential, most effective, and least expensive marketing technique available and you cannot succeed without it. Research indicates that consultants are often hired on recommendation. Networking is your primary means of making your skills known to potential clients.

A contact network is a collection of acquaintances and people to whom you have access and who will facilitate your entry to organizations and people for whom you wish to work. The greater the number of people in your network, the greater your chance of success.

Don't worry if your circle of friends and associates seems narrow. You probably have a large network that you have not activated. Furthermore, networks are not static; if properly cultivated, they grow geometrically. This chapter will tell you how to recognize networks, how to develop contacts, and how to cultivate connections.

Principles of Networking

- The networking habit: Networking will continue as long as you are in business. If you wish to succeed as a consultant, incorporate networking into your life. Internalize the procedures this chapter presents until they become automatic. You can meet people who might be helpful to you anywhere.
- Being "used" is a compliment: Those who are unfamiliar with networking may feel they are "using" people, which is true. But the dynamics of the relationship are much more complex than you may think. When you cultivate a new contact, you recognize another individual as a person of power and influence. In our society, in which what a person does reflects what he is, it is flattering to be recognized as noteworthy, a person of consequence.

- Favors: You cultivate a contact because he will be somehow helpful at another time. You expect to ask that person a favor. It is understood, although you shouldn't say so, that you, in turn, will be helpful to him in the future. While you must exude helpfulness, it will rarely be used. Your contacts may not be as well-organized or as goal-oriented as you are. You have the advantage because you know what to do, where you are going, and what you want—attributes that most other people lack.

- Act first: Do favors for potential contacts in advance. These should be favors that involve little time, involve few resources, and are unexpected. One of the easiest favors you can perform is to pass on information, especially information that you cannot use and that can be shared without diminishing its value. Many people hoard information. This is foolish because the longer information is hoarded, the less valuable it becomes. This is discussed more fully in the section "Cultivating your network."

- Consultants are helpful: Performing favors for people does not merely create indebtedness, but also cultivates your image. If people think of you as helpful, they will think of you when they need help.

- Listen: A good consultant must be a good interviewer and listener. This is how he understands a client's problems. Listening is equally important in networking because it helps identify people who are needed for your network, it helps identify favors that will be most appreciated by a contact, and it helps to identify opportunities for contracts.

- Automatic acceptance: You will be meeting people in many social and non-business settings, in which your qualifications will rarely be questioned. A cocktail party or a professional gathering is not a job interview. Most people will not be aware that you are looking for work. If you start to explain your work or suggest that you can help with a problem, you won't be challenged. Your mutual acquaintances or membership in an organization vouches for you. Your honesty and capability are assumed, and you are assumed to be a peer. Therefore, if a conversation led to some mutual interests, neither of you would ask the other for a résumé. Instead, you might exchange business cards.

- Business cards: You must have a business card because it is your first introduction. The chapter "Getting Started" explains card design and production. You should present it at every opportunity, and ask for one in exchange.

- Collecting cards: Asking someone for a card is a compliment to them. When you receive a card, note on the back when and where you met the person, what you talked about, and other pertinent data. Keep these cards on file and use them.

- Maintaining records: You should also maintain a file of contacts. Note meetings, personal or professional information, and copies of correspondence (see samples section, p. 90)
- A lead is just a lead: Just because you have met someone does not mean that person will be useful to you or buy your services. Only about one in 20 contacts will result in a successful engagement. You will learn as you proceed which leads you want to cultivate, who will be useful, and in what way they will be useful.

Entering and Using Existing Contact Networks

You are part of at least one network. Tell everyone you know what you are doing, give them your card and send a brochure or a brief description of your service line (see samples). Those networks you are already part of or can easily join include:

- Family: Your family is your primary network. Few people know what their parents, siblings, aunts, uncles, and cousins do. Renew relationships with them because they may have connections that you can use. Let them know what you are doing and ask for favors or introductions. Unless your family is muddled by feuds, relatives will be happy to help you. They will be proud of you if you succeed, and proud to have been instrumental in your success.
- Current associates: Everyone you have worked with in the past or work with now is a professional associate. This includes individuals in other organizations with whom you do business. When you leave your job, especially if you are fired, let everyone know that you are leaving to establish your own business. Telephone or send them a brief note announcing your intentions. In the letter or an enclosure, include a service-line synopsis (see samples section, p. 108). This is crucial because if you do not tell people where you are going, people who telephone your former office will hear, "Mr. Jones is no longer with us." Do not allow this impression to live. If you do, you will be professionally ruined (see samples section, p. 94).
- Religious groups: National and international religious groups are networks that can be used to ensure your economic as well as spiritual salvation.
- Alumni organizations: Alumni organizations are personifications of the old-boy network. Join as many of them as you can; dues are usually low. Read their publications, especially those concerning alumni activities. Note who has been promoted to influential positions, whether they were members of your class or not. These people have announced their promotions because they want to be recognized. If you send them congratulatory letters, you will be doing what they want. Send

23

information about anything you are doing that relates to their activities (see samples section, p. 128). In the next chapter you will learn more about using alumni magazines to promote your activities. Go to alumni functions occasionally. They will connect you with many useful people. It is also a good way to contact classmates or professors who did not attend but would be helpful to you. Send a note saying you met a mutual friend or that you missed their presence.

- Schools: If you are in school or taking a course or workshop, get to know anyone who may be helpful to you and bring that person into your network. You should pay particular attention to the teacher of the course because he is likely to be the most advanced person in the group. You may take a course simply to meet a well-recognized teacher.

- Fraternal or sororal organizations: Fraternities and sororities epitomize the concept of the old-boy network. These organizations are often national or international and may publish newsletters or magazines that can be useful. These groups are not limited to colleges; adult fraternities, sororities, and clubs exist as social or civic associations (see samples section, p. 102).

- Civic groups: Civic groups are inexpensive to join and can acquaint you with notable political figures and other influential community figures. These associations often publish newsletters in which you can be featured. More details are provided in the next chapter.

- Professional organizations: Join at least one professional association. Almost all hold annual or semi-annual conferences, which you should consider attending. Do not go to all the meetings at the conference, but go to the bar to meet people. Invest some money in buying drinks for people. Approach wallflowers, and encourage anyone you meet to talk about themselves. Ask about their work, ask for their card, and offer yours. Follow-up appropriately. If you know someone who works for the same organization, ask if he is a mutual acquaintance. These organizations all have leaders. Concentrate your efforts on meeting those leaders and bringing them into your network. By establishing contacts with leaders, you acquire access to their contacts. Many organizations will also have publications that you can use.

- Tangential associations: Depending on your field, there may be a variety of groups you should join. For example, a graphics specialist might join a local contemporary arts museum or art society, and an urban planner might join a local historical society. You might even join a sports or social club frequented by local business leaders—a golf, tennis, country, or luncheon club. You may discover some informal networks.

- Mentors: If someone prestigious in your field takes you under his wing, consider yourself fortunate. A mentor can help you advance rapidly by vouching for you and introducing you to his network. Your mentor must have an excellent reputation to be of value. Enter the relationship with some caution, making sure you get along well with your mentor. Ascertain how the individual will accept your professional growth. Some mentor-disciple relationships end disastrously when the former begins to see the latter as a threat.

- Benefits: Most organizations hold widely publicized benefits. Allocate some funds, perhaps $100 a year, to attend these functions. Some are quite expensive, but others cost only a few dollars. Consider spending $25 or $50 to become a sponsor, but only if a list of sponsors will be published. There are sometimes receptions for sponsors at which you can meet some influential individuals. Do not attend these events alone. Bring a friend who is a skilled conversationalist who can look and act as a savvy socializer. If there is a bar, buy drinks for people. You can rise in someone's estimation by spending two dollars on a cocktail. Encourage people to talk and introduce yourself to leaders. Distribute and ask for cards, but do not distribute brochures. If you expect someone to be useful, follow up with a letter and appropriate materials. Gather any available material. Look for committee listings that will help you identify leaders.

- Lectures and workshops: Check local and city papers for announcements of guest lecturers or workshops. If you live near a college, your chances of finding presentations by well-respected experts are greatly increased. Attend sessions that will not draw a large audience because it will hinder you from gaining access to the speaker. Approach the speaker after the presentation to present your card and tell the speaker you would like to write him. Ask where you can reach him. Do not expect to have a long conversation with the speaker, even if there is a reception, because you cannot compete with the distractions that usually occur. If the speaker is being neglected, however, take advantage of the situation by acting as a host. If there is a reception, other participants may also be potential contacts.

- Mailing lists: Put your name on several mailing lists to receive a wealth of useful, free information. Mailings may advise you of less-publicized events, may profile leaders, and may identify an organization's problems, thus providing you an opportunity.

- Social and business pages: Read the social and business pages of newspapers. These columns concentrate on leading public figures about whom you should learn as much as possible.

- Sophisticated fan letters: Every field has its leaders whom you should know. If you lack the means of meeting these leaders, send a sophisticated fan letter (see samples section, p. 96). There are a few basic elements to a fan letter. The tone should be informal. You want to be perceived as a peer even if you are not. It should be brisk and professional. Include specific compliments about some aspect of the leader's work. Comment on an admirable book, article, lecture, or technique. Show that you are in a related field and that you may be a good addition to the leader's network and should be treated civilly. Enclose a few professional samples of your work. Do not enclose anything amateurish or handwritten unless you specialize as a calligrapher. Do not ask to become acquainted, but later to meet. After you receive a response, decide on your next move. There is a greater chance of receiving a response than you might expect. Leaders appreciate this type of flattery. Fan letters needn't be limited to leaders. Consider sending letters to professionals in your field, newspaper columnists, editors, authors, legislators, candidates, public officials, anyone you can compliment for a job well-done, and people who don't usually receive recognition.
- Employment ads: Read the help-wanted ads. When you notice a listing that specifies skills that you have, respond as if you were interested in the position. You are not looking for the job, but are interested in getting inside information about the company, making friends inside the company, and acquiring a new client. If you get an interview, you should not reveal that you are a consultant. Act as if you are considering the position. Ask questions about the company that can be used in future consulting assignments. Identify problems for which you can provide solutions. Ask very specific questions at your initial meeting. The interviewer may be more open during this meeting than at any other time because he does not perceive you as a threat or a member of a faction. He expects a professional applicant to explore business conditions carefully before committing himself to a job.

If you get a second interview, tactfully reveal that you perceive needs that you could solve as a consultant. Explain with diplomacy why you feel the company's interest would be better served by hiring you as a consultant. Do not press the point, but introduce it. Tell the interviewer you will present some ideas in writing. Suggest that after the position is filled, there may be some services you can provide as a consultant that the chosen applicant cannot. Remain cordial and follow up on your suggestions.

Cultivating your network

These activities will lead to an extensive contact network. You will have to keep in touch with people and keep relationships active because contacts take some time to mature. There are a few means of accomplishing this.

- Congratulations: If there is any reason to congratulate a member of your contact network, send a brief note (see samples section, p. 98).

- Progress reports: If someone has been helpful to you or shown interest in you, inform them of your milestones. Send copies of articles by or about you. If you changed, added a service, or developed a new brochure, send those changes to people who should be kept up-to-date.

- Pass on information: Unexpected favors are greatly appreciated. If you notice an article that may be of interest to someone else, pass it on with just a brief note. If you learn of a business opportunity or a useful connection or have an inside line on political events that could affect members of your own network, let them know. Be discreet, however. If the event is only rumored or pending, pass that on also. Do not be perceived as an unreliable gossip. Information need not relate to business. For example, if being on a mailing list brings news of an art exhibit that one of your contacts would enjoy, pass on the mailing or send a note.

- Entertaining: Entertaining is one of the best means of staying in touch with and doing favors for several people at a time. Plan to have about four cocktail parties a year. As a consultant, you should conduct these parties somewhat differently from your previous parties. First, the party can be a success even if nobody comes because you will invite people with whom you wish to keep in contact but with whom you cannot spend much time. Your invitation itself indicates that you are thinking of them and are willing to do something for them. You may prefer intimate dinners or wild beer blasts, but cocktail parties are less expensive and more conducive to mixing than dinners. They are more sophisticated and more conducive to conversation than keg parties. Your guests will appreciate a party because few people can now afford to entertain. But people enjoy parties as much as ever; your invitation is valuable.

If your home is large, centrally located, and attractive, hold a party there. If your home does not qualify for any of these reasons, consider renting a function room. A restaurant or hotel may be beyond your means, but you may find an inexpensive, presentable hall at a fraternal organization, civic center, or college. Send invitations at least three weeks in advance. Invite a group of friends and associates who you see regularly, who think well of you, and who will speak well of you. You may ask a few close friends to help you host the party. Ask some people whom you have not met, including local people to whom you have written fan letters, especially the leaders in your field, political or community leaders, and media professionals. Do not worry about inviting too many people. Everyone will not come, and everyone will not appear at once. You will be very busy during the party, so arrange to have hired help or close friends to take care of the bar and food. You must be free to greet people and make introductions. Your role is as facilitator. If you have invited associates or sub-contractors with whom your clients will work at some time, introduce them. If it would be beneficial for one member of your network to meet another member, introduce them to each other. For example, you may introduce a potential client to a satisfied client. Or you may have a prestigious friend or associate who would impress a new contact. One of your guests may want to meet another. There are myriad opportunities at parties to do favors for people. Don't forget the wallflowers and people with whom you are trying to cultivate stronger ties. There are always two keys to a successful party: plenty of liquor and plenty of interesting people. Have enough of both. Invitations, liquor, and hors d'oeuvres should cost about $250. It is a worthwhile investment and a valid business expense.

A final note about networking. Do not neglect your peers. Develop a group of people who are working in closely related areas, preferably not in direct competition with you. Consulting is unique, and you will feel more comfortable having a group of people around you who have chosen this lifestyle. The shared characteristics that brought you to consulting will often be conducive to good friendships. These people will be helpful in several ways. You can share resources, contacts, concerns, and information. If you have difficulty with a client, or experience a crisis, your peers can support you. If a group already exists, they may welcome you as a member. If not, form a new group. During networking, you will meet peers. If they are interested in creating or joining a group, suggest meeting for lunch or cocktails on a regular basis.

CHAPTER IV

MARKETING AND PROMOTING: SELLING YOUR EXPERTISE

Regardless of how well you network, there are limits to how many people you can reach. Networking is only one marketing technique you can use to develop a clientele. "Marketing" is a very general term, covering any activity that ultimately effects sales. It includes advertising, publicity, distributing materials, public appearances, educational services, and planning related to promoting yourself or your product line. It also includes analyzing your market, negotiating, and making actual sales. Selling merchandise includes special techniques, such as coupons or sales. But you are selling expertise. A consultant is inseparable from his service line. Rather than concentrate on selling services, concentrate on promoting yourself as an expert in your specialty.

Like networking, marketing and promoting oneself must be incorporated into your life. They are on-going activities, not one-time experiences. You are your own agent. You may feel awkward about marketing yourself, but it should become automatic with practice.

You and all your marketing efforts must project an image. You must project:

- Knowledgeability: People are paying for your expertise.
- Authority: Others must perceive you as an authority.
- Directness: Your client must know that you have no doubts about your recommendations or skills.
- Candor: You will often be commenting on delicate situations; your clients must feel you will be honest.
- Personableness: Your client must see you as someone who is easy to work with and talk to.
- Selectivity: Even if you are desperate for work, keep up the image of being highly selective about your clients. Give the impression that you are honoring a client by taking an assignment.

All your materials must have these traits to be successful marketing tools.

Standard marketing tools and technique

- Service-Line Synopsis: The easiest marketing tool to produce is a brief 300-to-500 word description of your service line. It is a preliminary brochure. It should be an itemized listing rather than a narrative so that it can be read quickly.

• Brochure: Almost every service business has a brochure, and you should create yours as soon as possible. It should be concise and easy to read, it must highlight the functions of your business, answering any commonly asked questions, and it must be written in a positive tone. It should not make comparisons to other businesses, be adversarial, or quote prices. One of the easiest, least expensive formats to work in is an 8 1/2- by 11-in. sheet folded in thirds to form six panels. The outer panel or cover should feature the business name, address, and telephone number. If the name of your business does not indicate a type of service, include a descriptive sub-title. The first inner panel should begin with a brief (25- to 50- word) description of you, what your business is, and what organizations will benefit from your services. Divide your service line into its main functional areas and use these as topic headings. For example, the first brochure for my fund-raising consultancy had three topic headings: fund-raising and organizational development; federal funding opportunities; and lectures, seminars, and workshops. Under topic headings, list your services and itemize them for easy reading. Business executives will dispose of any brochure that cannot be read quickly (see samples section, p. 110).

Reserve a panel, usually the one that folds in, for capsulized biographies of the staff or associates. These should include a list of: colleges and degrees, honors, articles or books, teaching, and other pertinent information. If you lack a partner and staff, indicate your range of associates, specifying their fields. Do not include their names, particularly at first, because your associates are likely to change. If, after you have been practicing for a while, you have developed a firm relationship with associates, offer capsule biographies of them on an insert that is the same size as a panel. You may include a partial list of clients, but only if they are prestigious. The remaining outer panel should be designed as a business envelope so you can send the brochure as a self-mailer.

The brochure must be well-produced because it is your envoy. The design should be simple, clean and professional. Keep design costs low by asking advice of someone in your network who is knowledgeable about public relations or graphics. However, don't expect this person to do your brochure for free. You must have it typeset and printed, not typed and xeroxed. Typesetting costs range from $50.00 to $100.00, and most typesetters and print shops will do the art work for a nominal fee. If you use one color and simple graphics, offset printing should cost only $2 or $3 per hundred copies. There are additional charges for high-quality paper, art that is difficult to reproduce, and colored inks. Keep your original artwork. If you change some copy in the future, you can re-use your originals. Do not invest a lot of money in your brochure, particularly at the beginning because it may change. Your brochure will not bring business. People expect a brochure, just as they expect to be served water in a restaurant, but, like the water, a brochure is not nourishing. It is only a step above a business card and an introduction that lists your service. The first brochure legitimizes your business. Later, you will rely on other materials. Until you have those materials, send your brochure as a follow-up to new members of your network or as an announcement of your business to people you know. It will help them define your business.

- Case Studies: Many consultants prepare 50-to 500-word case studies, project descriptions, or abstracts of their assignments. A case study could list your projects on one or two pages to give the range of your services, or could offer one or two case studies that directly relate to services you are trying to sell to a potential client. Concentrate on the techniques used and the benefits that the client received. It might be necessary to keep client names confidential, so the description should cite only the types of business rather than names (see examples section, p. 104).

- Direct Mail: Whether you have worked as a secretary or as a top executive, you have probably received direct-mail announcements on a wide range of services and products. But most direct-mail packages are thrown out, particularly if they are not addressed to a person. The response rate on direct mail is rarely high enough to cover the extensive costs of a purchased list, printing, and postage.

The more well-targeted your mailing, the more effective it will be. Send your brochure to people you know and those with whom you can claim an affiliation. For example, if you belong to a professional association, you might send your brochure to other members with a brief letter explaining that, having just joined the association, you would like to introduce yourself to the other members (see samples section, p. 102). It should be addressed to a specific person. If you have a list of organizations that are likely to use your services but with which you do not have contacts, use that list, but personalize your letter. Find out who your letter should be addressed to by telephoning the organization and asking the receptionist who the appropriate person is. Send only as many letters as you can follow up --perhaps three to five per week. State in the letter that you will telephone within 10 business days, and do so. There are several free lists available from trade associations and publications, the chamber of commerce, and government. You can also purchase lists from brokers. Dun and Bradstreet sells computerized listings at fairly reasonable rates. These lists are useful to you only if you personalize and follow up your mailings. You can expect 10 letters to yield about one interview. This seems like a low rate of return, but it would be even lower if you do not personalize and follow up your mailings.

- Paid advertising: Advertising, the most widely used means of providing news about a service or product, is not a good route for a beginning consultant because it is extremely expensive. A beginner does not have the resources to compete with established businesses. In some fields, advertising is illegal; in others, it is considered unethical or in poor taste. If you must advertise, select a publication that is targeted to your potential clients.

- Leave-behinds or advertising aids: Businesses sometimes offer their clients small gifts,such as pencils, pens, calendars, coin holders,or letter openers. These free gifts are emblazoned with the company's name and logo. If you decide to invest in such gifts, or "leave-behinds," make sure it is a reminder of the service you offer. Graphic artists and photographers, for example, sometimes create calendars illustrated with samples of their work. There is a direct relationship between their services and their leave-behinds. A computer consultant might create a mini-dictionary of common computer terminology or a real-estate development advisor might draw a map that indicates rental rates in various parts of town. Other types of leave-behinds, such as articles by or about you, project listings, or mini-case studies, can be mailed or presented when you cultivate a lead.

- Finders' Fees: Discreetly indicate to a few people in your network that you will pay a finder's fee if a lead results in a contract. A finder's fee is a commission, the amount of which is usually a percentage of the gross contract fee. Do not pay more than 10 percent of the contract fee, and do not pay until the contract is signed. Tell the finder in advance how much you will pay. It is a great incentive to get someone to do your marketing for you.

Innovative Marketing and Public Relations

The standard techniques described above, with the exception of the brochure, can be quite costly and are not strongly recommended. Many innovative, effective, and inexpensive approaches to publicizing your services, however, do exist. In certain cases, you will be paid rather than having to pay. These approaches are targeted toward building your reputation as a leading expert in your field.

Client References

Use client references aggressively in seeking new business. Don't wait for a client to ask for references. When discussing an engagement with potential clients, insist that they consult satisfied clients on your services. Offer references of clients who had similar problems to those of your potential client. Your client must give you permission to use his name as a reference. Pose this request in a flattering manner, making it seem like an honor. When you give clients' names for references alert them, so that they will expect the call. Do not ask for written references, but save any letters praising your work. Most people are more willing to spend time on the phone than to write a letter.

First Engagements

If you are leaving to a 9-to-5 job and have never consulted before, you may have difficulty convincing people that you are qualified. Some ways you can begin to build a clientele include:

- Moonlighting: While working your 9-to-5 job, hunt down a few engagements. If your contact is someone connected with your job, you may need your employer's permission before accepting the engagement. Asking permission is of less concern if the contact originates from another network, but some employers have specific rules regarding moonlighting. You may have to accept a lower fee for a moonlighting engagement because of your reduced availability. Do not create a conflict of interest.

- Using your current employer: You may be able to convince your employer that it would be worthwhile for him to hire you as a consultant rather than as a regular employee. You will risk your position by presenting this idea and should be prepared to leave soon after, regardless of the employer's response. This transition can be difficult, and you should attempt it only if you have a good relationship with your employer. Having been an employee, it is difficult to rise to the authoritative position of a consultant. You must be considered exceptional in your organization, and you must have the complete confidence of your employer. The best circumstances under which you can attempt this transition are when you are an organizational maverick and when the organization cannot offer you room for advancement. In that case, your employer may see that the only way he can keep you is as a consultant.

- Volunteering: If you cannot manage the above methods, volunteer to consult to some organization on a specific task, for a specific time period. Make it clear from the start that this is a limited offer and that you are doing this in exchange for a reference. Take on the most sophisticated task you can, for the most prestigious organization you can get into. Do not bite off more than you can chew. If you are quite sure of yourself, aim for a top level position in a nationally known organization such as the Red Cross or the American Cancer Society. A nonprofit business will receive you better than a for-profit business. If you are not confident of your abilities, volunteer to a medical clinic or day-care center. Volunteering is a waste of time unless you do your job well. Treat it with the respect you would give a paid engagement. Very often a volunteer position can be parlayed into a regular assignment.

Exploit the Media

- Using media: Editors, news directors, and programming planners sometimes have more space or air time available than their regular staff can fill. Chronically understaffed, they rely a great deal on outside materials. Take full advantage of this opportunity to publicize yourself.

- Using announcement columns: Alumni, professional, and trade publications usually have announcement sections that are fairly easy to get into. The business pages of daily newspapers often have a similar section but entry is more competitive. Send an announcement when you begin practice and periodically update it with announcements of milestones, such as publishing a book or an article, receiving an award or an honorary position, presenting important lectures, and adding to your service line. Write the announcement in the same format that the publication uses and make sure to identify your affiliation with the publishing organization, including year of graduation or membership in the professional association (see samples section, p. 128).

- Writing articles: Write about four articles per year that directly relate to your service line and expertise. Getting an article published is third-party recognition. If the publication regards you as sufficiently expert to contribute, then the readers will also (see samples section, p. 118). Identify all the available outlets where an article by you might be well-received, such as trade publications, professional publications, local newspapers, or local magazines. Carefully research these publications to familiarize yourself with the type, format, tone, and style of articles they print. Ask your librarian for help and check the most recent edition of *The Writer's Market*, an annual directory of publishers. Many publications will provide writer's guides on request. Decide how your ideas or materials will blend with theirs. Your article must be newsworthy: it must offer new information or a new angle on an old idea. If you have difficulty generating ideas, watch major events in the news. You can also telephone editors, particularly of small publications, and say that you have an idea that you would like some help in developing. Arrange an appointment or talk on the phone. The editor may not be particularly interested in your idea, but he may identify articles that he wants written. It may be worthwhile for you to write an article slightly outside your specialty for the sake of future receptivity from the editor.

If you have a well-developed idea, send a query letter to the editor—the standard means of asking an editor if he is interested in an idea or article. Send it to a specific editor, and use his name if possible. It should include: the idea and why it should be of interest to readers; your qualifications; a specific format, length, date of availability, and the next step you will take; for example, state that you will telephone in 10 days. The letter must be well-written and concise—no more than one or two pages (see samples section, p. 114). If your idea is accepted, it will be on speculation. The publication will not promise to pay for or print the article until it is deemed suitable and timely. Do not expect to be paid very much. Some professional journals don't pay at all or pay only moderate honoraria. Local newpapers usually pay $15 to $25 for a short piece, and the regionals and major dailies pay as little as $1 and $2 per column-inch. You may eventually build a reputation, and your articles may become more valuable, but for now, think of this as an investment in your reputation. If you don't write well enough to produce publishable articles, work on your writing skills. In the meantime, hire a free-lance writer. If you do not have a writer in your network, contact a local publicity association or journalism school, which has names on file. The least expensive way to work with a writer is to draft an article and have him rewrite. Or, outline the article and have a taping session with the writer, explaining the details you wish to cover. This typical independent contractor relationship follows the rules detailed in the chapter on contracting. Do not tell the publications editor about your writer, and do not allow any contact between the two. If the editor wants some changes after seeing your submission, take careful notes and pass on the comments to the writer. Most writers are paid on a per-project basis for rates that start at $50 per day. Make it clear that you retain all rights to the article and any fees that result. When your article is published, make copies of it on your stationery. Make sure the name and date of the publication are on the reprint. You may also be able to obtain reprints from the publisher, especially if you are not being paid for the article. Distribute the article to anyone who might have interest in it, and use it with your sophisticated fan letters, new contacts, or old contacts. Offer it as a leave-behind to potential clients with whom you are discussing engagements. Your name, address, and telephone number should be on every piece of material you distribute, and it must be neatly pasted up and printed.

- Using articles about you: Every consulting profession has news value. Try to have articles written about you or that quote you. Suggest a news angle related to your work to an editor of a publication. For example, when the Reagan administration began, I contacted newspapers regarding the impact of budget cuts on nonprofit fund raising. Cultivate relationships with editors and reporters covering your specialty. If you have a relationship with a free-lance writer, offer your idea to him. He can do a lot of the legwork.

Your best chances for articles about you are with local newspapers. Trade or professional journals will probably be more receptive than general newspapers or magazines. National magazines are the most difficult to gain entry to because they demand a national news angle. Build toward these publications. When an article about you is published, use it in the same way you use one you have written (see samples section, p. 126).

- Press Releases: If you have accomplished something notable, such as filing a bill, publishing a book, or developing a unique service, you can get yourself published by writing press releases. Editors cut press releases from the bottom, so make your most important points first. When you plan an important event or lecture, send a press advisory to appropriate editors and reporters, letting them know time, place, and nature of the event. Address these releases and advisories to a specific individual or they may be lost. Expect to follow up on a specific release with telephone calls (see samples section, p. 124).

- Letters to the Editor: When a publication has carried an article related to your work or there is a news event or issue that you can expertly comment upon, send a letter to the editor. This is often a good way to break into a publication.

- Radio and Television: Talk shows are constantly looking for guests. Decide which programs are right for you and figure out an angle that would interest them. Telephone the station and find out who should receive the material. Expect to follow up on materials with a call. It is difficult to gain entry to television news. You must have a very strong case to present and, preferably, a visual angle. Radio and television appearances are not as beneficial as published articles because you cannot make copies of TV news reports, and few people remember the news. However, ask the station for transcripts of your broadcast printed on its stationery. Also, if you know you will be a guest on a show, advise members of your network in advance. They are not likely to tune in, but you will make the point that you are newsworthy. If you appear regularly, include it in your capsule biography.

- Lectures, courses and workshops: As your recognized expertise is widely confirmed, offer lectures or courses in your specialty. It is a means of heightening your visibility, promoting yourself, and furthering your image as an expert in your field, and it will help you identify people who are interested in what you do. If you are nervous about public speaking, start out by making a guest appearance in someone else's course because the audience is limited, and a classroom is less threatening than a hall or an auditorium. As you gain confidence, make yourself available to various groups in the community,such as the Rotary Club and the League of Women Voters. You probably will not be paid for your appearance, but if you are a good speaker, you eventually will be able to command an honorarium. Arrange to speak to audiences that will include potential clients or other professionals in your field. Professionals are probably more difficult to address, but addressing them is part of establishing your leadership in the field. You can offer courses at private or public continuing adult education centers or community colleges. Teach adults, not undergraduates. Through teaching, you'll meet clients and professional people who may become members of your network. Use samples of your own work, where appropriate, for course materials. When you teach, get the names, addresses, telephone, and business affiliation of all attending. Add these to your list of contacts. Follow-up by sending a brochure or other publicity materials to your audience. You may eventually offer courses, lectures, or workshops outside an institution. These programs are often in affiliation with a college or profesional association. Workshops can be profitable, but they require a substantial investment in developing a curriculum, materials, and marketing. You may begin by offering courses to your client's employees at their site (see samples section, p. 112).
Routinize lectures and course as much as possible, so you do not have to prepare for each one. However, consider customizing your presentation for each audience. Adults resent instruction that is irrelevant.
- Photographs: Include photographs with publicity materials, especially press releases, circulars about workshops, and entries to announcement columns. A photographer in your network might offer his services for less than a studio does. Copyright laws on photographs are specific and complex, so make it clear that you are buying reprint rights or the negative of a photo. Photographers typically charge more for duplicates than does a commercial reproduction business. Prices vary substantially, so shop around. The media and most printers prefer black-and-white 8- x 10-in. glossies.
- Books: Write a book on your specialty. You may be able to sell an idea to a regular publisher or an educational publisher. Some trade associations and magazine publishers also issue books within their fields. You can also publish your own book,

just as I have published this one. Do not use a vanity press. A local printer charges less. To be of use, a book must be well-publicized and marketed. You may wish to contract a distributor to handle the publicity and distribution of the book. A distributor will take up to 60 percent of the cover price, and a bookstore will take 40 percent.

The details of publishing and marketing are beyond the scope of this book; I will refer you to some "how-to" books listed in the bibliography. Books can be effectively marketed through direct mail. You need not buy lists from a broker because there are many free lists available in trade publications and from the government. Lists can be found of all libraries, human service organizations, and public agencies. Check the chamber of commerce, the economic development office, umbrella associations such as the United Way, and professional associations.

CHAPTER V

ONE FOOT IN THE DOOR: FROM LEADS TO CONTRACTS

The previous chapters will help you develop your product line and the types of organizations that will use your service. Through networking or marketing you will meet someone who can use your help, or you will find a client. Now, turn that lead into an engagement.

Your first connections will probably come through your network rather than through marketing. You will meet someone at a party or conference and discover an opportunity. Write to that person or to the most eminent person in his company, telling him that you have ideas you would like to discuss. Include in the letter any materials you have that relate directly to the topic. Call for an appointment within a week, and note the date on your calendar. It is important to follow up your promises.

Meanwhile, gather as much information as you can about the company and the person you will meet. Discreetly question people in your network about the firm. Check the business press for articles on the company and on related problems in the industry or business. Look up the names of the officers in Standard and Poor's Register of Corporations. Ask the company to send you brochures and annual reports. Learn as much as possible about the organization's structure, operational style and methods, products, markets, competitors, and problems. The more knowledgeable you are, the more respect you will gain.

During the first meeting, act as a facilitator, a concerned friend, or a colleague who wants very much to help. Do not sell yourself or prove your qualifications, because if you have met this person through your network or been introduced by a friend, you are already accepted. Don't act like a door-to-door salesman who intends only to unload a set of encyclopedias or a brush. Act instead like a physician who is seeking information about a patient before making a diagnosis and writing prescriptions. Be forthright, sympathetic, and helpful—never arrogant. Expect this executive to perceive you as an expert. You will help him with his problems by asking the right questions, not by boasting about yourself. Bring a checklist of questions into the meeting to help you pinpoint the problem, determine the executive's attitudes, and offer a proposal and contract that is directly targeted to the problem, the executive, and the company. Questions you should ask include:
- What do you see the problem to be?
- When did you first become aware of it?

- Has it become worse?
- What are its dimensions?
- What is it costing the company?
- How long do you think it will take to solve?
- Are there any internal obstructions to its solution?
- How do other officers in the firm perceive the problem?
- Has the company tried to solve the problem?
- Have you contracted with other consultants?
- What skills do you think will solve the problem?
- Will the company cooperate in solving the problem?
- Are there any external factors of influence?
- Are the competition, vendors, and general public aware of the problem?
- Are there any related problems that indicate a more fundamental difficulty than the one we are discussing?

Pick the executive's brain for the information you need to write a cogent proposal. Encourage him to present his viewpoint regarding the problem's solution. Consider his perspective and reflect it in your proposal. During conversation, he will probably refer to some documents related to the subject. If they aren't offered, ask if he has any materials that shed light on the subject. He will probably share them with you because you have presented yourself as a trustworthy helper. Ask if you can take these documents with you or if you can have copies. This material will provide you with additional information and decrease the amount of background work you will have to do.

In addition to seeking facts, watch for hidden messages about the executive and his management style. If the executive is task- and result-oriented, and wants quick results, be pragmatic, business-like, and stay within the defined areas. An autocrat requires an accommodating, respectful response, while a muddler looks for guidance and probably requires patience. A people-oriented executive wants a warm, idealistic response. When you offer solutions, they must solve the problem in a way that is acceptable to the administration and organizational system.

During the interview, the executive may ask how you will solve the problem. Do not say exactly what you have in mind because you have not yet been paid. Respond with an introductory response such as: "You've shown me the dimensions of an extremely intricate problem. I've had experience with this type of problem, and I would like to consider it seriously. I'll put my thoughts on paper and send them to you within a week." Send your proposal as promised. Postpone questions regarding references, qualifications, fees, and how much time the project will take. Discuss those subjects last.

Before closing the interview, promise to send your ideas at the end of 10 days. This is an ideal turn-around time. During that period, check the veracity of some of the information you have been offered by discreetly discussing it with people in your network or by checking it against industry literature.

The Proposal

There are certain basic precepts to keep in mind in preparing your proposal. A proposal is not written in cement; it is flexible. It includes your suggestions about the problem and its solutions. Any proposal carries an implicit counter-proposal; expect one to be forthcoming. You will succeed with your original proposal if you account for the needs and expectations of the other party. Do not expect your proposal to be accepted in its entirety. As you become more sophisticated at negotiating, interviewing, and analyzing the hard and soft data you gather, you will be more able to write a proposal that will meet the other party's expectations.

The proposal, in the format of a letter or memorandum, should be typed neatly and professionally on your stationery. It should usually be only one or two pages long. It must be clear and succinct. The person you send it to will circulate it and may have to sell you to others in the company. If you send an unprofessional document, you will put him in the uncomfortable position of having to defend your qualifications. He probably won't bother, and you will lose the account.

If you use a memo format, it should begin as follows:

TO: (The other party, by name and position)

FROM: (Your name)

DATE: (Date sent)

RE: (The matter being proposed)

Every proposal should include the following elements:

- Title: a direct, one-sentence topic heading of what you propose.
- Project Description: A 50-word synopsis of what you want to do.
- Purpose: A brief statement of who or what will be served by the project.
- Need: Describe the most compelling reasons that anyone might be interested in the project. This section is crucial if you have conducted your interviews well. It should echo the statements made by the contracting party during those interviews. Repeat the exact words he has used to assure yourself of a sympathetic hearing. If the person you send it to must defend it to others, he will be defending his own ideas with full commitment.
- Suitability: Why should this organization carry out this project? In some cases, the reasons will be implicit, and you need not detail them.
- First step: The first proposed step should be a tangible one that can be accomplished with little delay and that involves you. If it is complicated, you may dishearten the potential contractor. For example, suggest you interview other executives or convene to discuss the parameters of the topic. State that you will attend this meeting as a consultant, implying that you expect to be paid.
- Time: Estimate how long the first stage of the project will take. Do not underestimate the time, because you may find it difficult to change your estimate once the proposal has been made. Always allow yourself about a 20 percent margin. On the other hand, do not inflate your time requirement because a client may have difficulty justifying the expense required for a lengthy project. Be specific about the amount of time you need for each step. Time parameters for each step will serve as milestones later in the project. If a project will take five years to complete, do not tell the potential client your estimate. Your goal is to be hired; if a project seems immense, you may deter a client. Your first proposal should cover only the first stage, a manageable one. If the engagement goes well, suggest subsequent stages.
- Future steps: You may suggest subsequent stages that imply your involvement. This should be included only if you expect it will be well received.
- Consultant's relationship: Indicate in general terms how you will be involved. Do not state specific terms, such as 4 days at $500 per day. Explain your tasks, stating, for example, that you will have a managerial role, gather information, write a report, or interview personnel.
- Cost: Cost should be negotiated at a future time, unless you are quite certain, from comments made during the interview, that there is substantial interest in the project, and that the potential client is waiting for some written information. In that case, the

entire proposal should be equally specific. If you expect further negotiations to take place, you may have difficulty changing the financial terms to meet the new demands a company may place on you.

- Follow-up: State your next action on this proposal, stating, for example, that you will telephone within 10 business days. Note the date on your calendar. Mention of a follow-up can be included in a cover letter rather than in the proposal.

If you use a memo format, include a cover letter. Thank the party briefly for his cooperation and time during the meeting, highlight the topic discussed, state that you can help because you have experience with this type of problem, and flatter him in some way, mentioning, for example, that you found the discussion fruitful or that his analysis of the problem was acute. State when you will telephone next.

You may suggest in your cover letter that the party contact some of your other clients to discuss similar work that you have performed. If you offer references, you will familiarize the potential contractor with your way of working. You may do this later if you expect negotiations to continue.

For some projects or clients, include additional material with the proposal, such as relevant articles, samples of your work, or case studies explaining your procedures and methods. In some fields, proposals are expected to be packed with boiler-plate descriptions of previous experience and résumés of all associates. Do this only if it is standard in your field. A prospective client is usually put off by a stack of secondary information (see samples section, p. 130).

Standardized Proposals

To routinize and manage their work, consultants often develop a standard proposal or a series of proposal modules that can easily be adapted to create a semi-customized proposal. Each standard proposal or each module constitutes a service in the consultant's service line.

There are advantages and disadvantages to this approach. From the client's viewpoint, a pre-packaged plan indicates that other organizations have successfully used your methodologies and procedures. Your track record indicates that you can handle problems that relate to those of the potential client. The client knows what he is getting. He knows he will pay a set price for each service. Furthermore, standardized or modular proposals can be developed only after a consultant has fairly substantial experience. It reflects your image as an acknowledged expert.

On the other hand, many clients object to pre-packaged plans because they do not believe such plans respond to each organization's problems. Each company believes itself unique, and might be insulted at the implication that they are no different than other organizations. One common complaint against consultants is that they apply a standard solution to every client, regardless of individual characteristics.

From a consultant's viewpoint, routinization is essential because you cannot re-invent your service line for every new client. By standardizing your service line you know what to do, when to do it, how to do it, how much time it will take, and how much you should charge. You can write a proposal in just a few hours, instead of a few days. You can anticipate your work load and income over a longer time period, and you can provide better service.

Developing a standard service line does require experience and analysis. As you carry out your first engagements, note your procedures or methods, figure out how long each step takes, and analyze the similarities among projects and the average time invested in each aspect of an engagement. Note unique problems and barriers to implementation. Create modules to handle both unusual and common problems. You will change your modules or standard proposal as you develop new skills or services.

Standardized proposals or modules carry a set fee, which will cause change in negotiating. In customized proposals the fee is usually the major point to be debated. With standardized proposals, you may negotiate on minor details, such as how much clerical support the client will provide and whether incidentals, such as travel expenses, will be covered.

Proposal Follow-up

When you send your proposal, note in your calendar the day you promised to call; preferably, 10 business days later. When you call, try to arrange the next appointment. The following scenarios include the most likely responses to your proposal. These are neutral or negative responses. If your proposal is well-received, arrange the next appointment. If your first interview was on April 1st, mail your proposal on April 15th, and telephone on the 29th.

You: Hello, Bill. Did you get the proposal I sent?
Prospect: Yes, but I haven't had the chance to read it.
You: All right, I'll call you back in a couple of days and we can discuss it.

If he hasn't read it, call back in two days, on the 1st of May. (Don't attempt to explain the proposal if he hasn't read it yet.)

You: Hello, Bill. Have you had a chance to read the proposal?

Prospect: Yes, I have. I'm circulating it to some individuals. I'm really interested myself. It looks fairly promising. I'll get back to you in a week.

You: Okay, if I haven't heard from you in a week, I'll call you on May 6th.

Note the date on your calendar, and, if you have not heard anything by then, telephone again.

You: Hi, Bill. Have you discussed the proposal with your colleagues?

Prospect: Yes, but I'm afraid they feel we should discuss it further before we decide whether to proceed.

You: Then I'll get back to you in 30 days. Will that be enough time?

Prospect: A month seems sufficient.

You: Fine, I'll call you on June 6th.

Make a specific date and note it on your calendar. On June 6th, telephone again.

You: Hello, Bill. I was wondering if you and your staff have made a decision regarding the proposal I sent.

Prospect: Yes, but it isn't something we're interested in right now.

You: I'm sorry to hear that. I was looking forward to working with you. I hope that something can be worked out because I'd like to follow the situation and see how it develops. I'll call you in two or three months to find out how things are going.

By September 1st, call again and, if possible, start the procedure over again. Even in a worst-case scenario, don't drop the contact. Promise to call again, and do not be negative or hostile.

Should the prospect, during the call, respond positively, arrange an appointment to complete the negotiations. Avoid negotiating on the phone because you cannot present your best case or ensure that money is the prospect's last consideration while on the phone. You also cannot read the prospect's facial and body-language signals, which indicate how he is receivng your comments. Unless your client is desperate and you are are holding all the cards you should not negotiate on the telephone.

Negotiations

The primary purpose of negotiating is to settle the differences between your proposal and the prospect's counter-proposal. Anticipate this counter-proposal. Negotiations are composed of: 1) What you want, 2) What you must have, 3) What your client prospect wants, and 4) What your prospect must have. Every item in a negotiating session falls into one of these categories. Your ability to define each point will assist in your move to resolution and to a contract that both parties can live with. It is extremely important to negotiate an agreement that leaves both parties satisfied.

As you begin negotiating, form an idea of how each negotiating point will fall into these four categories.

Maintain a confident mien during this session. Assume that a contract will be signed and that it is not a matter of whether you will work for the company, but of when you will begin. Be helpful, positive, and ready to resolve minor differences, so that you can begin working as soon as possible.

Determine the extent of the other party's interest in hiring you. Probe with indirect questions, such as: "Has the situation gotten worse or improved?" You can then determine how much the organization needs you.

Next, determine how your proposal has been received. Ask if it is acceptable as is or if it requires changes. If there is general acceptance, work toward a contract and settle on specifics. Leave the meeting with a clear idea of the services you will provide. These services, which are abstract in the proposal, must become concrete and detailed. The client's responsibilities must also be clearly defined. Sort out the categories of "What you want/ What you *must* have" versus "What the client wants/ What the client *must* have." Mentally prioritize these.

Suppose the client and you have difficulty agreeing on a point. If he asks you to perform services you did not intend to perform but don't mind including, make it clear that this will lengthen the project and, hence, your fee. If he asks you to perform a task you don't want to do yourself, subcontract it and allow for increased costs. If you want no part of a task, say so. Some consultants use the tactic of raising the price to a very high level, and assuming their opponent will back down, and then having the opponent agree to the exorbitant fee. This can lead to sticky situations. If you are backed into a corner or cannot come to an agreement on a point, proceed with other aspects of negotiations and make an agreement on most of the contract. Get a substantial agreement. Although it is better to resolve everything in one session, sometimes that is impossible. Make it clear that you are certain a consensus can be reached, plan another meeting, and leave on a positive note.

Usually, the most difficult point on which to reach an agreement is your fee. This is easier if you use standardized contracts with a fixed price for all services. If so, you will probably spend more time negotiating on the details of responsibilities.

Some general tips on negotiating include:
- Be sure your opponent has the power to negotiate.
- Maintain a friendly, positive attitude.
- Do not become querulous.
- Prioritize your needs.
- Allow for flexibility on minor points, not on major ones.
- Be well-organized.
- Don't compromise your major objectives.
- Know your opponent well and be as personable as possible.
- Do not sit in a diminutive position. That is, do not sit at a lower level than your opponent.
- Make sure the session will not be interrupted. If necessary, suggest that the door be closed and that the secretary hold all calls.
- Do not negotiate in public places.
- Do not drink during negotiations.
- Avoid negotiating with more than one person. If you must do so, however, control the meeting and sit in a prominent position.
- Rather than turn down an unacceptable suggestion, remain silent. Your point will be clear.
- Break tense moments by suggesting you move on to another point, stop for a cup of coffee, or lighten up the conversation for a moment.
- Disagree positively.
- Avoid last-minute changes in terms.
- Do not make a big deal about minor errors on either side.
- Be honest.
- Make sure you both understand the terms.
- Do not criticize others (consultants, firms, associates).

- Do not be cowed by your opponent's symbols of power or success.
- Dress and behave professionally.
- Avoid going off on tangents.
- Remain calm. Do not let your opponent know that either one of you has scored on a point.
- Find out immediately what the reasonable position is and co-opt it.

Setting Fees

Consultants charge for their services in several ways. Your daily rate is a base on which project or retainer rates are determined. Some consultants work on a commission basis or accept various "in-kind" or benefit payments.

Determine the typical rates in your field to set up your rate. The Department of Labor's Bureau of Labor Statistics may help you determine how much full-time employees are paid in specific geographical areas. It may also have statistics on consultants, but a better source of information is the other consultants in your field because you will be competing with them.

If you have difficulty determining your daily rate, use this rule of thumb. Divide your top annual salary by 52 and then by five, giving you your highest daily pay rate. For example, if you earn $15,000 per year, your weekly pay is $288.46 and your daily rate is $57.69. For your minimum daily consulting rate, multiply that figure by 2.5 and round it off, giving you a daily rate of about $150. Multiply by 2.5 to account for expenses you incur in doing business. Employers normally assume that benefits, such as paid vacations, sick leave, insurance, and social security account for one third of an employee's pay. If you earn $15,000, your employer spends another $5,000 per year to cover your benefits. Account for overhead and marketing time also. An average of only 14 to 17 days a month is billable. The rest of the time is spent marketing, improving your skills, and doing administrative work. So, if you charge $150 per day, bill 15 days per month, and allow four weeks of vacation, you should gross about $32,000 per year. You will pay all your operating expenses out of that, and you will pay 8 percent in social security on the net income. An unusually high overhead will reflect those costs. Some expenses are negotiable, and those are covered in the chapter on contracts. This rule of thumb is applicable only at the beginning of your consultancy. You can increase your daily rate substantially within six months or a year.

Another rule of thumb is that consultants generally do not charge for less than a half day. If you spend only two hours with a client, you charge for half a day. On the other hand, if you put in a 10-

hour day, you charge for only one day. It is uncommon for consultants to charge hourly rates. Project fees are based on the number of days you expect to put into a project. If you estimate a project will take five days, including your 20 percent leeway, charge five times your daily rate ($115 x 5 = $575).

When you begin practicing, you are not likely to be hired on a retainer because it implies that the client cannot do witout you. When a client wants to pay a retainer relationship, base the fee on the amount of time he wishes to reserve. If, for example, the client wants you to be available approximately one day a week, the monthly retainer fee will be four times the daily rate. You will be paid that amount whether they use that time or not. If the client needs more of your time, bill at your regular rate.

Commissions and in-kind payments are fairly unusual, although they are standard in a few fields. Fundraising solicitors and proposal writers are often paid a percentage of the funds raised. If you promise to increase an organization's profits, charging on a commission basis assures your client of full commitment. It can be difficult, however, to assure yourself of the client's full commitment or to force them to pay you once the money is raised. Consider a commission if a company is in dire straits and cannot pay an up-front fee. In that case, you might also consider in-kind payments, such as company stock or goods.

In either case, you gamble that the company will make a recovery. In-kind payments or benefit packages are sometimes used to keep taxable income lower or to gain access to a service or facility that you would have to pay for at substantially higher rates. If, for example, you work for a company that has a health club, you could negotiate that part of your payment is membership in that club. Such an arrangement is legally taxable and should have a dollar value assigned to it. However, it is very difficult for the Internal Revenue Service to trace, thus, some people do not report it as income.

If you work on a long-term project that lasts for more than a few weeks, arrange for interim payments. A project that will take two to three months requires one-third payment up front, one third halfway, and one-third on completion. Longer projects can be billed monthly or according to agreed-upon milestones. They can also be billed at a lower rate than short-term projects because you need not invest time in marketing. On the other hand, you might raise the price for one- or two-day assignments. Consider the client's quality. If you want to get a foot in the door of a prestigious company, lower your rate. However, if your rate is too low, your credentials might be questioned. Some consultants moderate their rate according to the difficulty of task and the level of skill needed. If a client is known to be uncooperative or delinquent in payments, raise your rate to reflect the risk of accepting the engagement. Rush jobs can also carry an extra fee. It is commonplace to negotiate charity accounts at a lower rate—particularly if the account is a prestigious organization or one that has a powerful board of directors. It may be worthwhile, for example, to reduce your fee to a local ballet company if the chairman of the board of the company is also president of the largest corporation in the city.

Finally, whatever you charge, ask for what you want without embarrassment. Do not apologize for your fee.

CONTRACTS & SUBCONTRACTS: GET IT IN WRITING!

It would be wonderful if business were carried out verbally. We like to believe that the people we work with are honest and honorable and that a handshake suffices when making a business agreement. Such an agreement is legally valid, but if a court battle results, it will be one party's word against the other's.

A written document, produced in duplicate and signed by both parties, will not only protect you in a legal battle, but also will help prevent misunderstandings. Questions about responsibilities should be solvable on the basis of a contract. A contract should consider all contingencies for disagreement. It is generally in your interest, however, to be more specific when buying services than when selling them. Don't get involved in minutiae while fulfilling a contract, but do get the criteria for work you purchase as specific as possible.

As mentioned, all elements in negotiating a contract fall into one of four categories: 1) What you must have; 2) What you want to have; 3) What the other party must have; 4) What the other party would like to have. When you write a contract, these points should be clear. You don't want a contract to be refused because you want 25¢ per mile for travel and the client wants to pay only 20¢. As a rule, a contract should not have any surprises; it should be fair and agreeable to both parties. Forcing a contract on another party will hamper your working relationship.

Trying to trick a client into a contract by having him sign when he is intoxicated, drugged, or insane is not only unethical, but illegal. Such a contract would not stand up in court.

As a consultant, you need several types of contracts. Some mechanical details that apply to all contracts include:

- The contract should be typed, one-and-a-half or double-spaced, on your stationery.
- It should be prepared in duplicate so that each party will have a signed copy.
- Both parties should initial each page.
- It should have a brief title.

Letters of intent

A letter of intent is the simplest form of contract. It can be used for selling or buying services. It considers the interests of both parties. The letter's format is much like a standard business letter, except it is produced in duplicate and leaves space for each party's signature.

The letter should clearly define the terms of the agreement. Points covered should include:

- Services: If you sell services, your responsibilities should be stated loosely. You might state: "I will prepare a report regarding personnel grievances, based on interviews with employees." If you are sub-contracting for a report, you might state: ""You will prepare a 50-page, double-spaced document based on my interviews of 20 employees. The report must be suitable for reproduction and presentation to my client."
- Special considerations or contigencies: These include any factors essential to the project. Using the above example, you might state that all interviews will be kept strictly confidential.
- Time factors: The duration and/or due date of services and materials should be clearly stated. For example, interviewing will take place between April 1st and 15th and the report will be delivered on or by April 20th. If you sub-contract the report, allow time to review the material before submitting it to your client. Hence, you might state that the report must be submitted to you by April 17th.
- Payment: The rate and means of payment should be clearly stated. For example, the project will require four days at $200 per day, payable within 30 days of completion. If you buy services you might omit the payment due date, but the other party will probably insist upon one.

Close a letter of agreement with a request that the other contracting party sign and date the letter in a specific place and return a copy so that each party has a signed copy for his files. This letter constitutes a legal and binding contract (see samples section, p. 134).

General contract

A general contract is a somewhat more formal, detailed, and elaborate document than a letter of intent. Develop a contract that can be applied to all or most of your engagements and have it checked by a lawyer. You do not want to draw up a new contract for each project or to pay a lawyer's fee for each one. A general contract should include:

Title: Define the nature of the agreement in a few words.

Date and parties: Write the contract's date and the names of the contracting parties in the first paragraph. This paragraph usually specifies that for the remainder of the document, you will be referred to as the "Consultant," and the other party will be refered to as the "Client."

Introduction: Most contracts include a brief statement regarding the primary function of your business and the reason the client is contracting you. The wording should be general. For example, "Whereas Consultant is organized to assist non-profit corporations in fund-raising activities; and Whereas Client is a non-profit corporation interested in purchasing the services of the Consultant, Now, Therefore, it is agreed between the parties as follows:" If your business is a corporation, this line may be taken from your charter.

Services to be provided by Consultant: Be as general as possible in defining your responsibilities, but do not be so vague that there is no substance to the contract. State that you will meet regularly with the client, rather than stating a specific time. Use abstact terms, such as "advise," "review," "prepare," and "assist" rather than more concrete statements. Your client might want clearer terms because the more specific the contract, the more control the client has over your work. Include in this section any activities that you must perform to serve the client. If you must perform a task anyway, you should get credit for it. Review any prior efforts made to resolve the client's problem and include that task as one of your services.

General conditions: Points that should be covered in this section include:

- You, as a consultant (or corporation), agree to use your best efforts to perform the services identified above. This is a promise of your good intentions.
- The client allows you reasonable access to his place of business, books, staff, and records to allow you to perform your services, and that the client agrees to cooperate in providing them.
- The client is responsible for all reasonable disbursements the consultant makes on behalf of the client. That is, the client will reimburse you for expenses. Specify these items, including travel and accommodations, long-distance telephone calls, copy costs, postage, and anything else you expect to pay for while servicing the client. If you omit an item, you might have difficulty getting reimbursement. For example, you would not usually charge for office expenses, but if you use a typing service to prepare a report, you must negotiate with the client on who is responsible for that expense. The contract should specify an amount above which you must have the client's approval to make an expenditure. A ceiling of $10 or $15 should be assuring to the client, although it may be

$50 or $100. State how you will bill the client for expenses and the terms of payments. For example, state that expenses will be billed on the first of each month and payment is due within 30 days. You may want to include contingencies for late payments, as described below, under fees.

- Depending on the type of services you provide, you may include a statement regarding future rights to materials generated during the engagement. For example, if you write a report, that report will continue to be your property. Your client may argue this point; it is negotiable. If the client refuses this point, aim for getting credit on the materials. That is, your name should appear as the author of the report or that your company prepared the report for the client.
- If appropriate, include a statement regarding a guarantee. For example, one of my general contracts specifically states, "Both parties hereby acknowledge that no guarantee of funding is made by the Corporation to the Client."

Client's responsibilities: In most cases, the client will provide only those items specified above. However, this section should specify any agreement the client has made to provide you with office space and clerical support, or to perform activities you need to do your job.

Fees: Clearly state how much you will be paid, how you will be paid, and contingencies for late payments. If, for example, you charge a project fee of $6,000 and expect the project to last six months, spell out the details, such as whether the client will pay you $1,000 on signature and an equal sum on the same date each month, whether he will pay you in three equal installments, or whether you will bill the client.

Your statement regarding late payments could read: "If any payment, as per the above schedule, is more than 30 days in arrears, the client hereby authorizes the consultant to charge the client a one and one-half percent penalty on the amount in arrears."

To protect yourself against more serious delays, add this statement: "If any payment, as per the above schedule, is more than 60 days in arrears, Client hereby additionally authorizes Consultant to declare the Client to be in default of this agreement. In such an event, the Consultant may, in his sole discretion, declare the entire unpaid total of payments owed in this agreement immediately due and payable."

If an engagement ends in a court suit, you will want to be protected against having to pay legal fees, or costs. Include in your contract a statement that the client is responsible for court costs and lawyers' fees resulting from the settlement of the contract. Expect some surprise from your client on this point. Nobody wants to enter a contract expecting a court suit. Explain that your lawyer has advised you to include this statement in all contracts to protect your interests. Point out that this clause would be applicable only if the client fails to pay the fees they have agreed on, thus placing the onus on the client. Assure the client that you do not want the engagement to end in a court battle.

Termination: You could include an escape clause in any contract, but it is particularly important for commission contracts because the performance of the client has a direct impact on your earnings.

Conclusion: The concluding section should include: duration, meaning how long the agreement will remain in effect; entirety, which means the contract is complete as written and can be amended or modified only by a written agreement signed by both parties; applicable law, covering the state whose law governs the contract (for example, "This contract is to be construed as a Massachusetts contract"); and signature, include the date, a line for each party's signature, and a line for the title and organization of the other party.

Variations

If you work on a commission or retainer basis, the wording of your general contract will differ from that of a general contract.

Commissions: A commission contract must spell out the client's responsibilities in greater detail than do other contracts because you rely more heavily on the other party's performance to profit from the engagement. In "General Conditions" or in "Client Responsibility," include a statement permitting you access to any correspondence, memos, or records that document client income on which you may take a commission. In the "Fees" section, specify all funds that might result from your effort after the contract is outdated. For example, if you write a proposal that is used a month after the contract has ended, you are eligible for a commission. Or, if a three-year grant results from a proposal you have written, you receive a commission on the funds received by the client in the second and third years of the grant, even if you no longer have a contract. This section should include the commission percentage rates, but it must also state the time alloted between the day the client receives funds and the day you will be paid. State specifically that you will be paid in 10 or 30 days; the client could withhold the money as long as possible.

A termination clause can be included in any general contract, but it is particularly important in commission contracts because the consultant depends more heavily on the client's cooperation to earn his fee. If a client does not cooperate, you will need an escape hatch. Balance this with a client escape clause. These should be written before the concluding section.

Commission contracts are risky for consultants. Do not work on commission alone. Instead, include a basic consulting fee to be paid at the commencement of the contract (see samples section, p. 142).

Retainer contracts

Contracts involving retainer fees differ from general contracts only in the fees section. Cover the amount of time alloted to the client under the retainer fee, the method of billing and payment, and the contingencies for work exceeding the agreement. Your client might want you to specify rates for additional work, so be prepared to advance the figures.

In-kind payments: If you will be paid in-kind with goods or services, the "General Conditions" or "Fee Section" of the contract should specify who will be responsible for appraising the value of those goods or services.

Workshop contracts

Many workshops are offered in association with colleges. The relationship and contract differ substantially from a typical consulting relationship. The basic elements should include:

Introduction: Title the contract and open with a paragraph stating that you and the other contracting party will co-sponsor a workshop.

Parties: Include the name, incorporating state, and principal place of business of each party.

Relationship of parties: The other contracting party employs you or your firm as an independent contractor to provide the professional services or products outlined in the contract. You may want to indicate that this agreement does not bar you from providing a similar service to any other organization.

Duties of the parties: Specify in this section all the responsibilities of each party, covering the following elements:

- The contracting party will co-sponsor a workshop on a specific date (or dates) at specific times.
- The contracting party will promote the workshop in a specified manner.

- You will supply the other party with appropriate publicity materials at a reasonable time before the workshop.
- The contracting party will provide a hall and the appropriate equipment (microphone, projector, etc.), personnel to process registration and introduce the workshop leader, and, if appropriate, lunch and the personnel to serve it.
- You provide the specific materials used in the workshop.
- Specify whether you will be the workshop leader or will provide a workshop leader. The other party might resist your bringing in another individual as the leader, so this point should be made clear during the negotiations.

Registration, attendance, and fees. This section should cover:
- Who will participate? In addition to the registrants, the co-sponsor may be allowed a specific number of free admissions.
- Number of registrants: Most workshops are limited to a specific number. While you do not want to limit your potential earnings, consider how many people you can effectively address.
- Fees: Vary the fee, depending on whether lunch is served or encourage pre-registration by setting a higher "at-the-door" fee.

Consideration and deductible expenses: Because the other party collects the registration fees, spell out the details of your payment, covering:
- The percentage distribution of net proceeds to each party.
- Your minimum payment. Cite a minimum that covers your investment of time and materials.
- The definition of net proceeds, meaning all registration fees minus itemized deductions.
- Deductions should include travel, accommodation, meals, transportation, publicity, workshop materials, and lunch expenses.

If you have contracted someone to run the workshop, deduct travel and accommodation expenses for him. You may not want the other party to know the terms of your sub-contract with the workshop leader, so allow for the leader's fee in the distribution of net proceeds and the minimum payment.

Withdrawal, cancellation, notice, damages. Plans for a workshop can fail for several reasons. Protect your interests in this section, covering:
- An acceptable manner of presenting withdrawal notice.

- A deadline, typically 30 days, before which a party can cancel without incurring damages to the other party.
- If a party cancels after the deadline, the other party must be paid liquidation damages of a specified amount (25 percent of your minimum fee). An exception to this would be severe weather conditions or a natural disaster, in which case the workshop can be postponed to a mutually agreed upon date.
- If a workshop is postponed or cancelled, the co-sponsor will bear the costs of refunding deposits or fees to registrants.

Assignability, which covers the rights of both parties to assign or delegate responsibilities, is meant to assure the co-sponsor that you will not bring in another workshop leader.

Applicable law specifies under which state law the contract is written.

Integration is the same as "Conclusion" in the general contract and covers entirety, amendment, date, and signatures.

Independent Contractors and Subcontracts

As your consultancy grows you must hire other people to work for you. These people enable you to handle more complex projects, to serve more of your clients' needs, and to get more business. In some cases, these people will work directly for you by writing an article or a brochure, keeping books, or typing reports. In other cases, you will give them work from your contracts with clients — sub-contracting.

Build a network of people who may potentially work with or for you. Do not wait until you need someone before interviewing; rather, create a pool of resources with the expectation that you will expand. Anticipate your needs and your clients' needs and watch for people to meet those needs. Just as it is worthwhile for you to find a mentor when you start out, it is also worthwhile to cultivate new talent. Novices will work for a fairly low fee because they are eager to prove themselves. If they are upwardly mobile, they may gain positions of power and be indebted to you. You are likely to work with peers whose skills differ from yours. The relationship can be mutually beneficial because you introduce each other to new work opportunities. Some of them may eventually become your associates, but that relationship is for "tried and true" consultants, not newcomers.

These people are not just your employees, but independent contractors, just as you are an independent contractor, not your client's employee. The nature of your relationship with someone you hire must be absolutely clear. An independent contractor does not receive such benefits as social security payments or workman's compensation. You should not be burdened with providing these benefits, nor with the extensive paperwork they require. There have been several court battles on the question of what constitutes an employee versus an independent contractor. Many employers avoid providing benefits by calling their employees independent contractors and treating those contractors as employees. The line between the two can be quite fine. The difference lies primarily in the degree of supervision allowed in carrying out the work. Here is the IRS definition of an employee:

> Under common law rules, every individual who performs services that are subject to the will and control of an employer, as to *both* what shall be done and how it shall be done is an employee. It does not matter that the employer allows the employee considerable discretion and freedom of action, so long as the employer has the *legal right* to control both the method and the result of the services.

> Two of the usual characteristics of an employer-employee relationship are that the employer has the right to discharge the employee and the employer supplies tools and a place to work.

> If you have an employer-employee relationship, it makes no difference how it is described. It does not matter if the employee is called an employee or a partner, co-adventurer, agent, or independent contractor. It does not matter how the payments are measured, how they are made, or what they are called. Nor does it matter whether the individual is employed full or part-time.

> No distinction is made between classes of employees. Superintendents, managers, and other supervisory personnel are all employees. Generally, an officer of a corporation is an employee, but a director is not. However, an officer who does not perform any services, or performs only minor services, and who neither receives nor is entitled to receive any pay is not considered to be an employee.

This is the IRS definition of an independent contractor:

> An independent contractor is a person who contracts to perform a piece of work *according to his or her* own methods or judgment. This finished product of his efforts, but not the means used, must conform to the employer's specification. Normally, an independent contractor has the right to employ other individuals, either regular employees or independent contractors, to complete the contracted work.

If you hire someone to do your typing regularly, and that person can choose his own hours or can pass the task on to someone else, that relationship qualifies as an independent contract. If you insist the typist come to your office at a specific time and work under your supervision, the courts would probably interpret that as a regular employer/employee relationship.

Deciding to Sub-Contract

The intent of the law is to provide a measure of protection for employees; when a case comes to court, the court is more likely to rule that the individual is a regular employee and entitled to benefits. Make sure your relationship is clearly defined and mutually acceptable to both parties.

If you subcontract, decide on how much contact will be allowed between the independent contractor and your client. Your client should believe you do all the work yourself because he pays for your expertise and may want to pay less if someone else does the work. You need not mention that you are using a sub-contractor nor explain your relationship with your associates. However, if you are directly asked, do not mislead the client. In some cases, it will be obvious that you sub-contract some work. And sometimes, contact between an independent and your client will be necessary. You may be questioned about a sub-contractor's qualifications; be prepared to respond, but make it quite clear that you are fully responsible for the quality of the work performed.

A sub-contractor, on the other hand, may try to take advantage of access to your client to sell his services directly. You can protect yourself by writing a non-competitive clause into your contract with an independent. Consultants who regularly use independents sometimes write a general contract, separate from any project, defining their relationship and the independent's relationship to the consultant's clients (see samples section p. 144)

You are responsible for the work you contract for, regardless of who performs the tasks. Allow time for review when assigning due dates to sub-contracted work and submit the work on your stationery rather than the sub-contractor's.

Setting fees for sub-contractors can be fairly complex. You may pay 20 to 80 percent of the amount allocated to that task in the general contract. That is, if you have a $500 contract to prepare a report for a client, and you have figured typing and editing that report at one-fifth the cost, or $100, you would pay the subcontractor $20 to $80. The more experienced you are, the greater percentage you will take. The sub-contractor pays you to market and to be associated with you. Sub-contractors resent high-markups on their service, but large consulting firms frequently charge their clients as much as four times the amount they pay their own personnel for the work. When writing a sub-contracting contract, the elements to consider include:

Title: Briefly state the nature of the document, i.e., "Contract for the performance of independent contractor services" (see samples section, p. 144)

Introduction: The opening paragraph states that the document is a contract between you and the other party, referred to as the "contractor," and includes the business address of each party.

Parties and relationship: This section should define the relevant aspect of your business, the contractor's capabilities in relation to the specific project, and an independent contract relationship clause that states that the contractor is not an agent or an employee of your company.

Duties: Explicitly define the contractor's responsibilities. Detail due dates, work quality, and other agreed-upon qualifications. In assigning due dates, allow sufficient time to review the work and make necessary corrections before the work is sent to your client.

Consideration and payment: Be specific in this section. If you pay a per diem rate, state the number of hours per day and the amount paid for fractions of days. This section should also cover responsibility of the parties for any expenses incurred. Anticipate claims for expenses.

Cancellation: You do not want the other party to cancel a project in mid-course, leaving you unable to fulfill the agreement with your client. However, you do want to be able to cancel if your client does. This section should state that the contract is not subject to cancellation unless your client cancels. It must include a statement regarding payment for work done upon notification of cancellation. That is, you should pay the agreed-upon rate for the work already completed at the time of cancellation.

General conditions: This section should cover confidentiality, ownership rights, and competition.

In this section on confidentiality, acknowledge that the contractor has access to information about you or your company and about your client. The contractor must restrict his use of that information to the performance of the duties described in the contract. This is negotiable and should be clarified before entering into a contract.

The competition clause should define the relationship between the independent and your client. The independent may negotiate strongly on this point because he wants few limitations in selling services. The contractor typically agrees not to perform his professional services for your clients, unless you employ him to do so, for two years after the termination of the contract. In some cases, the restriction applies to potential clients within a geographic area. For example, if you train an independent to lead a workshop that you have developed, the contract may restrict the person from offering that workshop independently anywhere in the country, within certain organizations, or within the part of the city in which you work. The more restrictive the clause, the more resistant the independent will be to it.

Applicable law: This clause defines under which state's law the contract has been written.

Assignability: To assure that the contractor is the only one who will perform designated duties, state this in the contract.

Term of Contract: This clause states the duration of the contract.

Integration: As with the other contracts described, this section covers entirety of the contract, means of cancellation or amendment, date of signature, signatures, and titles.

CHAPTER VII
GETTING STARTED: SETTING UP SHOP

Consulting usually requires minimal capital investment and low overhead expenses. It is important, however, that you spend your money well. Your office, stationery, and answering service should enhance your image. Everything your clients will see should bespeak prestige, confidence, capability, and experience. Invest as much as you can in the accouterments of your practice.

Selecting a name

Select a name for your company that will serve you well for an indefinite time. Avoid calling your business guild, shop or any type of pun, because that practice is passé. Instead, use your own name and add "associates." As a consultant you sell yourself; your business name should promote you. If you are not incorporating, you can do business under you own name with a minimum of red tape. If you have a common name, such as John Smith, or a complex name that people will not remember, you might also select a name that describes your business, such as "Communications Associates" or "The Educational Advisory Service." The name should be general enough to allow development of your service line. A photographer, for example, would not want to limit himself with the name "Family Portraits" because it would prevent his business from growing into commercial photography. Nor should you call yourself a free-lancer; in today's business world it is unprofessional. Whatever name you choose, especially if you incorporate, check with the Secretary of State to make sure you do not infringe on another company's name.

Locating an office

You will probably begin working in your home. The only reasons to rent an office when you start are barriers to working at home, such as inaccessibility to clients or a houseful of small children. You should have a separate room for your office because you need privacy to work and because the IRS discourages deducting expenses for a multi-use room. If your business is a corporation, it can rent a room from you more easily than renting square footage. Furthermore, your consultancy will intrude on your private life; you should leave your office and business behind during off-hours.

If you are well-located, have an attractive home, and have no difficulty with family interruptions, you may continue operating out of your home indefinitely. This is particularly true if you tend to visit your clients' offices rather than having them come to yours.

Do not rent an office until you can charge 70 percent of the expense back to your clients. If you rent an office, consider sharing a space with other professionals. A suite of offices with a central reception area can be more reasonable and attractive than a single office. It also enables you to share the expense of a secretary or receptionist and to purchase or lease equipment, such as a copy machine, that would otherwise be beyond your means. In selecting an office, consider accessibility, a prestigious address, rental rates, and lease agreements. Moving frequently is expensive and bad for the image of a stable business.

Your office should be attractive, comfortable, well-lit, and in keeping with a professional image.

Equipping An Office

Buy the best basics for your office that you can afford. Style should reflect both your taste and the type of business you do. A management consultant might have a leather-topped desk, while a commercial artist might have a more contemporary, utilitarian work space. It is a question of both image and practicality. Regardless of your budget or service, shop carefully. Both new and used furniture is expensive. If you have limited funds, consider used-furniture stores, and check the newspapers for bankruptcy auction ads, in which you can often find high-quality, low-priced equipment.

The basics of every office include:

- A desk: Consider the amount of work space and the number of drawers you need. Prices begin at $40 used and $150 new.
- Filing cabinet: Buy a cabinet with at least four drawers. Prices begin at $20 used and $80 new.
- Chairs: A good comfortable chair is essential. Prices for secretarial chairs start at $30 used and $60 new. They are best for long periods at the typewriter. Executive models start at $40 used and $90 new. Occasional chairs start at $10 used and $25 new.
- Book and utility shelves: Allow room in your office for your professional library and supplies. If you have a supply closet, you can use inexpensive, metal shelves. Prices begin at $20 used and $30 new.
- Typewriter: Invest in a good, self-correcting typewriter. The best ones sell for about $1,100 new and $900 rebuilt. Monthly rental rates are about $65. A four-year lease is about $50 per month, and about 65 percent of the payments can be used toward purchase if you decide to buy. Leases and rentals usually include service. Prices for typing tables start at $50.
- Calculator: What type of calculator you buy depends on your business. Pocket-sized

calculators sell for as little as $10; prices for business-function calculators start at about $30, and prices for desk-top printing calculators begin at $70. It is not advisable to buy used calculators.

- Tape Deck: A tape recorder can help you to keep reminders while you are on business trips. They can also double as dictaphones and be used in meetings and workshops if you do not want to take notes. Prices for standard portable models start at less than $30, not including a carrying case, rechargeable batteries, a plug-in microphone, and other options. If you expect to travel with yours consider investing $125 or more in a pocket-sized mini-cassette recorder.

- Dictaphones: Dictaphones can take standard or mini-cassettes, and some non-standard sized tapes. If you buy both a dictaphone and tape recorder, match cassette sizes. Prices start at $50 for a new unit. More costly models with foot pedal controls are worth the extra investment.

- Card file and/or address file: These are available in any office-supply store for $5 or more.

- Lamps: Lamps must fit in with the rest of your decor, but look for an adjustable style that allows for flexibility in lighting your desk, reading area, typewriter, etc. Models that clamp onto a desk sell for $20 and more and prices for floor models begin at $60. Used adjustable lamps are difficult to find.

- Clock: A consultant's time is money! Glancing at a conveniently placed clock is less obvious than looking at your watch. Prices begin at $5.

- Incidentals: You may want a wastepaper basket, a bulletin board, an easel, a chalk board, desk-top organizers, photographs, and other decorations. These items should enable you to work comfortably.

Business supplies

Your office should be well-supplied with notepads, pens, pencils, paper clips, and the like. You should not interrupt work flow because you run out of staples or tape. A good business stationer can provide you with note pads by the dozen and pens by the box. Do some shopping because prices vary substantially. But once you find a good store, stay with it.

Two supplies are particularly useful. First, buy a good calendar with plenty of room for notes regarding appointments, promised phone calls, and deadlines. Many calendars include address books and notepads. Second, buy a notebook to keep by your phone, rather than a message pad. The notebook can be a record of your calls and a convenient reference for names and telephone numbers, which may get misplaced if you use a regular pad.

Your business stationery - your card and letterhead — are most important because they represent you and enhance your image. Buy the very best.

Your letterhead should be clean, bold, and dramatic. It must include at least your name or your business's name; address, written without abbreviations; and telephone number(s).

It should be offset printed on white or ivory bond paper. Colored paper or ink can make unclear copies. Have envelopes printed to match. You might also want note-sized letterhead and envelopes. Purchase blank sheets, so your second pages will match the rest of your stationery. For drafts, copies, and some promotional materials, purchase lower-quality paper by the ream.

If you can afford $50 to $100, hire a graphic artist to design the stationery. Printers charge a lower fee, so get several estimates. Estimates should be based on the same quality of work and paper. Printing costs vary substantially, and can be arbitrary. Per sheet costs decrease substantially when you buy in quantity. For example, 100 sheets of high-quality letterhead sell for about $13, while 1000 sheets sell for $36. High-quality envelopes sell for $17 in 100-unit quantities and $57 in 1000-unit quantities. Many printers keep negatives on file, which lowers reprinting costs and is convenient to both parties.

Business cards typically reflect the design of your stationery, although this is not necessary. Many copy houses offer raised-print cards. A standard order of 500 is priced at about $15, but prices start at about $8. Printers will set the type or use your design. The more complex the design, the higher the price. The design may feature your name, the name of the company, your title, a short description of your service, such as "management and development for nonprofits" or "art investment adviser," your address, and your telephone number(s).

In creating stationery, you may consider a logo. Some corporations use their name as their logo, others use their initials as the base for their logo, and still others use a pictorial or an abstract design. A logo should be an immediately recognizable symbol of the company and it must, therefore, be strong, simple, and unique. Employ a good graphic artist to help you create one. Expect to pay at least $100. If the artist works on the the stationery and the logo at the same time he may charge less than $200 for both. When you adopt a logo, use it consistently on your cards, brochures, and distributed materials. Althought a logo is optional, it may be useful if your name is complicated and people have trouble remembering it.

You might consider buying adhesive address labels, which can be expensive, but are less than printing your name on folders or mailers. A rubber stamp serves the same purpose but lacks the professional flair that suits your image.

Services

- Typing and secretarial services: Plan to be your own secretary because you will have a substantial amount of correspondence and reports to prepare. Relying on outside help causes delay, inconvenience, and expense. Typing rates start at $1 per page, and they are higher if you submit handwritten drafts or dictaphone tapes. If you must type a draft, you can just as easily type the final copy. If you need a typist or a secretary for a special report or project, avoid using temporary employment services because they charge almost double what an independent charges. Good typists should be identifiable through your network. Many regularly employed secretaries will do extra work. Copy shops and colleges often have bulletin boards on which typists post information. Keep a file on record of good typists and their availability, rates, and specialities.

- Telephone services: You will need a telephone answering service because you will often be away from you office and do not want to frustrate clients who are trying to reach you. A reliable machine sells for about $200, although there are less expensive models on the market. The attachment that enables you to call your number and have the messages played back also sells for about $200. These machines are usually dependable, but many people dislike talking to a machine and will not leave messages. Personal answering services are also available. If your telephone district has call-forwarding service, you can hire a 9 to 5 service for $15 a month with little or no extra expense. The telephone company charges a small monthly fee for the service, and you must have a push-button telephone. If call-forwarding is not available, you might spend $15 a month but have a separate number for the answering service. Or you can spend about $35 a month for an extension of your telephone at an answering service.

There have been many improvements and new telephone services introduced lately, such as a signal that alerts you to an incoming call while you are on the line. This enables you to put the first party on hold while you speak with the second party. If you anticipate considerable long-distance calling, you might consider a WATTS line or one of the independent long-distance subscription services.

- Copying and printing services: In business and college areas, copying services are very competitive. Check price, delivery services, turnaround time and copy quality. Prices range from ¾¢ per page to 10¢ per page. If you need more than 50 copies of a page, consider offset printing rather than xeroxing because price for offset is usually lower, and quality is typically better.

  Printing services are also particularly competitive in price and service quality. If you expect to print large volumes of work for your clients, negotiate a commission from the printer.

- Insurance: If your personal insurance agent is part of a larger firm, he may have an asssociate who specializes in business clients. If not, look for a reputable moderately sized agency. A very large agency may not give good service to a small business, while an extremely small agency may not offer sufficient options. If you intend to hire regular employees, consider workmen's compensation. For yourself, consider disability insurance that will cover you if you should become unable to work. Some disability policies pay only if you are incapacitated—unable to work at all. Other types pay if you can not continue to work as you have been. Be cautious in selecting a policy.

A client may sue if your advice leads to disaster. Concentrate on protecting yourself in your contract rather than with insurance because premiums for this type of coverage can be exceptionally high. Property insurance is often accompanied by public-liability insurance. Property insurance covers your property in the event of theft, fire, and other risks. Some risks, such as earthquakes or hurricanes, are not included because the likelihood of these occurrences varies greatly in different geographical locations. Public liability protects you in the event that someone is hurt on your premises. If you expect to transport clients in your car or to hire a car and/or driver, you may want to buy additional car insurance. Personal health insurance can also be a problem when you are self-employed because rates for individuals are much higher than for groups, and some options are not available to individuals. Some professional and social organizations offer group plans to members. Insurance companies also vary substantially in their definitions of a group. Health insurance coverage and premiums are competitive, even in a geographical area that is dominated by few agencies. Shop around.

CHAPTER VIII

INCORPORATING

When you enter business for yourself, there is a tremendous temptation to form a corporation immediately because it underscores your decision and lends prestige to your consultancy. Incorporating right away, however, is usually impractical. A corporation, a legal entity with complex responsibilities and a great deal of red tape, can be expensive to form and to dissolve. It usually makes more sense to work as sole proprietor for at least a year to ensure that you will be happy and successful. The decision to incorporate should be based on a year of experience and on conversations with your lawyer and accountant. Meanwhile, operate with little or no added expense as sole proprietor.

Sole Proprietors

A sole proprietorship is the simplest form of business. It has no existence apart from you, the owner. Some cities and states require you to register your business in the city or town hall, unless you are working under your own name. You may have to find out whether your business is prohibited by zoning laws, or whether you require a peddler's or vendor's license.

In most circumstances, the only legality involved is filing the appropriate tax forms. The government counts your income, liabilities, and assets and those of the business as one. However, you should set up a separate bank account for your business. Financial records will be covered in greater depth in the next chapter. You will file and pay a quarterly estimate of your income tax and social security. You will also maintain records of business expenses and income. If you begin consulting while you have a regular job, the IRS will exact payment on your extra income.

Recent changes in the law have increased the attractiveness of sole proprietorships in terms of pension plans. As of 1981, you can deduct 15 percent of your income or $7,500 (whichever is less) for contributions to "Keough" retirement plans. If you are not concerned about retirement, you may wish to consider one of the these plans for the sake of tax benefits.

Depending on your income, there may be other advantages to being sole proprietor. For example, if taxable income is $15,000, the highest possible tax rate for a person filing singly with no dependents would be $2,352, or just below 16 percent. The lowest corporate tax would be 17 percent on the first $25,000. (These figures are based on 1980 figures.) If your income is low enough, you might save on taxes as sole proprietor. That is most likely to happen during your first year in business.

As a sole proprietor, you are least affected by regulations. Some states require a minimum working capital for corporations but not for sole proprietors. There are also the benefits of controlling your business directly, of minimal paperwork, and of reaping profits.

The greatest disadvantage of a sole proprietorship is that the owner has unlimited personal liability. In the event of a debt or a legal suit, everything you own is subject to claim. Another potential problem is obtaining loans, either for business or personal use. Banks tend to doubt the stability of sole proprietorships. There are also expenses that a corporation can deduct, but a sole proprietor cannot. For example, a corporation can own a car, pay health insurance, make contributions to charity, and own stock in other companies. Sole proprietors cannot take these as business deductions.

Partnerships

A partnership is a written or oral agreement between two or more parties to carry on a trade or business. In a general partnership, each party contributes money, property, labor, or skill, and expects to share in profits or losses. The term covers joint ventures, groups, pools, syndicates, or any other unincorporated organization, except for trusts or estates. The IRS says, "A joint undertaking merely to share expenses is not a partnership." For example, if you and some associates share the rent of an office, it is not a partnership. However, if you and an associate rent an office together and provide a service to other tenants in that office, it is a partnership. You must share in profits and losses to qualify for this category of business.

The benefits and disadvantages of partnerships are quite similar to those of sole proprietorships. Partnerships are legally easy to form, require minimal paperwork, are minimally affected by regulations, and, depending on the income, might offer a tax advantage over corporations. In certain cases, the liability of a partner may be limited to his or her investment in the partnership, but partners typically are fully personally liable in the event of debt or legal suits.

The greatest disadvantage of partnerships is the potential for conflicts among the parties involved. Partners share control over the business, but one partner's activities can legally bind the others. Personal disagreements hurt the relationship of those involved and the business. Resist the temptation to form a partnership, particularly with a friend. Business relationships often lead to good friendships, but friendships rarely survive a business relationship.

You can attain some advantages of a partnership while protecting against disadvantages by creating a limited partnership. This is most often used when an individual or business provides financial backing for a project but has no real involvement in carrying out the project. The limited partner would not be liable for debts or damages incurred by the other party or parties.

There is also classification for partnerships among doctors, lawyers, and some other professionals. These are regulated by state professional corporation acts.

Corporations

You may eventually decide to incorporate based on confidence in your success and on the advice of your accountant and lawyer regarding financial and legal benefits.

Advantages

- A corporation is a legal entity. Therefore, in the event of debts or legal suits, only the assets of the corporation are liable. By forming a corporation, you protect your personal assets.
- Corporations are taxed at a lower rate than individuals with comparable incomes, especially for incomes higher that $25,000. As of the 1984 tax year, corporations are taxed at the following rates:

Taxable Income Over—	But not over—	Rate	Of the amount over—
0	$ 25,000	15%	0
$ 25,000	50,000	$ 3,750 + 18%	$ 25,000
50,000	75,000	8,250 + 30%	50,000
75,000	100,000	15,750 + 40%	75,000
100,000	. . . .	25,750 + 46%	100,000

Incorporating becomes a tax advantage when you begin to make more money than you need for personal and business expenses. A corporation can elect to be taxed at personal income tax rates in some cases.

- A corporation has more options for financial planning. For example, rather than drawing a large salary from the business, you can have the corporation invest in the shares of another corporation. Eight-five percent of the dividends received are tax-free. A corporation can also accumulate earnings for future investment in the business. As of 1984, the IRS considers accumulation of as much as $150,000 to be reasonable.
- A corporation can provide an attractive benefits package. Health, life, and dental insurance; pension plans; company car; memberships in social or athletic clubs are frequently permitted expenses. N.B.: The IRS is bearing down on top-heavy benefit plans.

71

- Corporations can deduct expenses that a sole proprietor or a partnership cannot. For example, a corporation can deduct all bad debts and charitable contributions to as much as 5 percent of gross income.
- Corporations can raise nontaxable income by selling stock.
- A corporation has more prestige that an unincorporated business.
- If your business fails, the stockholders can claim part of the loss on their personal income taxes.
- As a legal entity, a corporation has greater continuity and transferability than an unincorporated business, which is useful in estate and family planning or in the event of a stockholders's death.

Disadvantages

The main disadvantages of corporations are that they require considerable expensive record keeping and a large monetary investment. You will probably need an accountant, a bookkeeper, and a lawyer. Most states charge corporations an annual $5 to $100 fee. If your business fails, declaring bankruptcy can be complex and expensive. The corporate shield against personal liability can be pierced in some legal situations. Banks might require the officers of new small corporations to assume personal responsibility for loans to the corporation.

As with partnerships, use great caution in forming a corporation with others, particularly friends. If you do so, try to maintain a controlling share of two-thirds of the stock. For the remainder of this chapter, however, I will assume that you will form your own corporation.

You can form a corporation without the assistance of a lawyer by purchasing a kit containing the necessary forms. These kits are available for $30 to $50 at business stationery stores. Registered agents in some states, notably Delaware, sell incorporating services for $25 or more. Some provide legal counsel for an additional fee. The advantages of incorporating in Delaware are covered later in this chapter. However, it is wise to consult a lawyer when incorporating. The $300 or so lawyer's fee is a worthwhile investment in peace of mind.

The Lawyer's Role

Use your network to find a good lawyer. Ask owners of small businesses if they know of lawyers who specialize in small businesses. Large, prestigious law firms cannot offer affordable, personal service. A young lawyer with a developing practice will be more readily available to you as questions arise and will charge lower fees.

You may find lawyers's approaches to billing unusual. Many request a deposit of new clients. If one is requested of you it means only that the lawyer is protecting himself against doing work without getting paid for it.

On the other hand, protect yourself against unexpected bills by determining in advance whether your lawyer charges a flat fee, an hourly fee, or a fee that reflects the benefit to you. Some prestigious law firms charge a dollar value on the results of their work. This fee may be shockingly high from the client's viewpoint. Another billing system is a contingency fee, which typically is charged to a client who is suing for damages or trying to collect unpaid bills. The lawyer is paid for out-of-pocket expenses, regardless of the outcome, and takes a percentage of the benefits the client accrues from the settlement or trial. Many lawyers work on a retainer basis for routine tasks or advice. If you have a good relationship with a lawyer, this might be the best route. The lawyer still charges for services or time beyond the scope of the retainer agreement.

Many states require a minimum of three people to form a corporation, although some allow one individual to hold all the primary offices.

If your state requires two or more people, your lawyer should become the clerk or secretary of the corporation so that he can maintain the records. He need not be a director just because he is the clerk. Although people often appoint close friends or family members as corporate officers, it is better to have people who work for you, such as lawyers or accountants, installed in these positions. This is because conflicts may arise between you and your family, and those conflicts may intrude on your business. If your state law requires a third person, consider using your accountant.

Your lawyer gets paid for any services provided in incorporating and maintaining the corporate records. It may be less expensive to do the preliminary work yourself and have the lawyer check it. Provide your lawyer with orderly and complete information so that you do not run up an enormous legal bill for work that is actually clerical.

Forms and Records for Corporations

Articles of Organization or Certificate of Incorporation: This form is available in kits available from the Secretary of State's office, some books (see bibliography), or from your lawyer. When completed, it should be sent to the Secretary of State's corporation department with the required filing fees. The certificate should include:

- The corporation's name: The Secretary of State will inform you if the name you have selected is unavailable.
- Location: This includes the state of incorporation and the address of the business. If you use a registered agent, his name and address are also included.
- Nature of the business: general language in defining the nature of your business. For example:

> To have and to exercise all the powers reserved for a corporation organized under and in accordance with the provisions of Chapter 156B of the Massachusetts General Law, and to do any or all of the things herein-before set forth to the same extent as natural persons might and could do, and in any part of the world.

Clearly define the main purpose of your business and the activities you intend the corporation to pursue. The clause above would close this section, following a more specific definition (see samples section, p. 173).

- Stock: The amount of authorized capital stock and if appropriate its par value.
- Name and mailing address of the incorporator: This may be your name and address or that of your agent.
- Initial Directors: State laws differ regarding the required number of directors. If possible, use only your name. Use your lawyer if necessary. Directors have power, so select someone who will not challenge your authority.
- Powers of the directors: The powers and rights assigned to directors usually include creating and amending by-laws, examining corporate books, managing capital stocks, specifying the manner in which the corporation's accounts are kept, fixing their compensation, and others.
- Officers: Standard officers include a president, a treasurer, a clerk or a secretary. Again, use only your name if possible and your lawyer's name if necessary. It is assumed that the names are the initial officers and directors and they can change in accordance with the corporate by-laws.
- Dates and signature: In addition to the incorporator's signature and that date, there may be spaces designating fiscal year and the time of the initial annual stockholders' meeting.

Record of initial incorporators' meeting: Before filing the articles of organization or certificate of incorporation, you must hold a meeting of the incorporators or make a statement of the action taken in lieu of the meeting. The minutes should include: The number of directors, the election of directors and officers, the adoption of by-laws, the date of incorporation, and the date of the fiscal year.

Minutes of Meetings: It is advisable, and often required by law, to keep minutes of your corporation's meetings, votes, resolutions, and other formal actions. This is true even if you are the only officer, director, stockholder, or incorporator.

By-Laws: By-laws set out the basic rules by which a corporation operates. Standard sets can be purchased as part of a kit or in a book, or you can write your own (see samples section, p. 156). Include these points:

- Section 1. By-laws and regulations of the business are subject to the provisions in the articles of organization or certificate of incorporation.
- Section 2. Stockholders: annual and special meetings, voting, quorums, actions by vote or by writing, and proxies.
- Section 3. Board of Directors: the number, tenure, powers, formation of committees, meetings, notice of meetings, quorums, and action by vote and writing.
- Section 4. Officers and agents: powers, election, tenure, and responsibilities.
- Section 5. Resignation and removal of officers and directors.
- Section 6. Vacancies on the board of directors and of officers.
- Section 7. Issuance and replacement of capital stock certificates.
- Section 8. Transfer of stock and methods of distributing dividends.
- Section 9. Indemnity of directors and officers: protects those parties, to the extent legally permissible, against the liabilities of the corporation.
- Section 10. The corporate seal, which can be purchased as part of a kit or separately from a stationer.
- Section 11. Execution of Papers: identifies the signatories for all legal transactions.
- Section 12. Closing day of the fiscal year.
- Section 13. Means of amending the by-laws.

Stocks

You will probably not be greatly concerned about distributing stock, but some options include:

Voting and non-voting stock: You can divide your stocks into two classes, with class A being voting stock and class B being non-voting stock. This could be a means of raising capital without allowing investors to control the business.

Command preferred stock: This is another way of dividing your stock. Preferred stockholders generally have priority over common stockholders in the distribution of dividends and assets but preferred stock often does not carry voting privileges.

With and Without Par Value: Corporations once assigned a dollar value to stocks, but this practice stopped around 1940. Now, most stock certificates represent a share in the corporation rather than a designated dollar value. You probably will not issue par common stock shares. Stock certificates can be purchased from a stationer. If you issue stock, you must maintain a record of the names and addresses of stockholders as part of your corporate records.

Variations On Forms of Corporations

Professional Corporations: Some states have laws governing associations of professionals, such as doctors, lawyers, and architects. Check with the secretary of state.

Sub-Chapter S corporations: If it is to your benefit, have corporate income taxed to shareholders rather than paying corporate taxes. This can be done at any time if you file a form (IRS 2553: election by a small business corporation) within 75 days of the beginning of the corporate tax year. To use this option, a corporation must be domestic, with one class of stock owned by no more than 15 shareholders. The shareholders must be individuals or estates and can not be non-resident aliens. The corporation may not be a member of an affiliated group.

Closely held corporations: State laws regarding close or closely held corporations differ. Check with the secretary of state's office. A close corporation restricts the number of shareholders and the transfer of stock. It usually requires that any stock being sold be offered either to the corporation or to other stockholders before anyone else is given an option to buy. Other restrictions or provisions concerning the sale or transfer of stocks and the management of the corporation can be written into the articles of organization or certificate of incorporation. Discuss this with your lawyer if you think it is appropriate.

Nonprofit corporations: The line between for-profit and not-for-profit corporations can be unclear. A not-for-profit corporation is typically formed for a civic advantage, such as artistic, educational, religious, or social service organizations. Professional groups, such as the American Medical Association or bar associations, usually are not-for-profit, as are civic groups, such as the League of Women Voters or Rotary clubs. The definition varies widely, and a corporation can switch from being a for-profit to being a not-for-profit, which was the case recently with *Ms.* magazine. Investigate this option because it offers substantial tax benefits. However, regulations that apply to non-profits often provide others with a large amount of control. A board of directors manages the affairs of non-profits. The members of the organization elect the board at an annual meeting. A nonprofit's assets must stay within the organization. Salaries and expenses can be paid, but the IRS may question exorbitant expenditures or salaries in an audit. You must apply to the IRS for tax-exempt status and usually file an annual report with the state attorney-general. If a nonprofit organization is dissolved, its assets must be given to other nonprofits. Tax-exempt nonprofits are also barred from lobbying, distributing propoganda, and getting involved in political campaigns.

Incorporating In Delaware

The state of Delaware has intentionally created laws that encourage businesses to incorporate. About one-third of the corporations listed on the American and New York Stock Exchanges are incorporated in Delaware. Some benefits include:

- One person can act as president, treasurer, secretary, sole director, and incorporator.
- No minimum capital is required.
- You can form the corporation by mail and hold meetings anywhere.
- There is no tax on business done outside the state and no inheritance tax on stock held by people outside the state.
- Delaware has a separate business court system that favors management and has a well-developed line of precedents that make legal matters predictable.
- Incorporating in Delaware may enable you to avoid paying your state's corporate income tax.

If you incorporate in Delaware, your state may require you to register as a "foreign" corporation and pay an annual fee of $5 to $200. Because Delaware has encouraged businesses to incorporate there, dozens of registered agents sell incorporating services. Their main service is to provide a Delaware mailing address, which is required for incorporation. They also sell legal services. Rates start at $25 for the address.

CHAPTER IX
BOOKKEEPING AND ACCOUNTING

Many new consultants are likely to regard bookkeeping as cruel and unusual punishment. It seems such a tiring, thankless task that most would be happy to go along without any records at all if they could get away with it! But your financial records are a useful tool for tracking the health and profitability of your business, planning investments, forecasting growth, and in keeping tax payments to the legal minimum.

Whether you are incorporated or not, start your bookkeeping by opening a separate bank account for your business. Incredibly, many consultants operate their businesses out of their personal checking accounts, which makes life difficult in tracking and controlling business funds.

You must be able to document all expenditures: this is the first essential rule of recordkeeping. You should do so by using checks and credit cards for payment. If you rely heavily upon credit cards, apply for a separate card for your business. If you pay in cash, save receipts and note what you purchase. If no receipt is available, document the expense in some way. You may find it convenient to note out-of-pocket expenses in your calendar, jotting down what you paid for and how it relates to business. Or, you might carry a note pad for this purpose. Frequent travelers should stock up on travel logs, available at a stationery store. Driver's logs are also helpful, particularly if you use your car for both personal and business reasons.

Bookkeeping

Even if you are good at figures, consider hiring a bookkeeper. A consultant's time is too valuable to waste on bookkeeping. While you can use anyone in your contact network to find a bookkeeper, you are best advised to ask your accountant for a recommendation because accountants and bookkeepers often work as teams. If your accountant can not suggest someone, consider these factors:

Bookkeepers specialize, but you will want a "full-charge" bookkeeper who knows all aspects of the job rather than someone who has specialized in, for example, payroll or accounts receivable. Your bookkeeper should be someone who can analyze figures, not just jot them down. He should be able to notice discrepancies in your monthly accounts. He should warn you when your expenses are rising disproportionately to your income. You must be able to rely on his discretion. Your books are private, and leaked information could be harmful to your business. The extent to which you use a bookkeeper will vary greatly, depending on the nature of your consultancy. At the beginning, a half or full day each quarter should suffice. If you work on many small projects, you might need monthly services early in your practice. Rates range from about $8 to $15 an hour, depending on your locality. It's worthwhile to spend more for a reliable worker. Mismanaged books can lead to difficulty and extra expense. You are ultimately responsible for providing the correct raw data and for overseeing your bookkeeper's and your accountant's work.

If you keep the books yourself, get some training. The Small Business Administration and the IRS offer workshops in major cities. Many high schools offer basic courses in the evening, as do many colleges, business schools, and adult-education programs. Various workbooks are available, including the Dome series, which is helpful and priced at $3 to $7. The basics of bookkeeping include:

Billing: Have a standard bill or invoice form printed or have each one typed as needed. Make multiple copies, for the client, one for your invoice file, and one for the client's file. Bills should have standard letterhead information, plus rates, terms, due dates, and other relevant information.

Document your billings. If you charge on a daily or hourly rate, maintain time sheets indicating the amount of time needed and the task performed. Many conultants use their daily calendar for tracking time, but if you are working on several projects at once it may be useful to create time sheets that fit into a ring binder.

Clients expect you to document expenses. Annotate all receipts so that you can prove that the expense was appropriate to your contract agreement. Bill for expense reimbursement separately because the funds received are not actual income.

To facilitate accurate, timely billing, set up two file folders. One holds unpaid invoices, and the other holds paid invoices. As invoices are paid, transfer the copy from one file to the next, noting the date of payment. Each month, check the "unpaid" file for outstanding invoices. Send the clients responsible for unpaid invoices a photocopy of the bill as a reminder.

Cash receipts journal: When you receive payment, deposit it in your business account, noting its source in your check journal. Keep a journal of your income in a separate book. If you have different types of accounts, use a columnar pad that will enable you to distinguish income from projects, retainers, hourly fees, book sales, workshops, speaking engagements, and expense reimbursement. By categorizing the different sources of income, you can use these records to determine the profitability of each activity. For each entry record the date, client, amount received, and the work covered by the payment. Distinguish reimbursements from income. This journal should be maintained on a monthly basis and reconciled with your monthly bank statement.

Cash Disbursements Journal: This is a record of your expenditures—how much you spent and on what. Purchase a "one-write" check book. If your bank does not offer this type of check-writing system, buy one from a bookkeeping- or accounting-supply house. Some checks you receive have a black carbon strip on the back. When the check is written, the entry is simultaneously recorded on a back-up page. This eliminates the need to write out the information again on a check stub and safeguards against your forgetting to record a check. These sytems come with a register divided into columns, enabling you to indicate into which category the expense falls. A system, including binder, checks, register and envelopes, sells for about $100.

Alternately you can transfer the information from your check stubs to a journal. The journal should include columns for date, check number, amount, recipient, and item or service purchased. Remaining columns can be headed as needed. Certain expenses, including rent, utilities, office supplies, copying, and telephone, occur monthly. Others occur only once or twice a year, so you need not hold a column open for them each month. Another system assigns a number to each account. When you record the expense, instead of disbursing the amount into columns, note the account number and tally all expenditures in that account at the end of the month.

By distributing your expenses across accounts, you can keep track of how you spend your money. They might help you determine when to subscribe to special long-distance telephone services, to purchase a copying machine, or to hire a secretary.

Balancing your checkbook: If you maintain good cash receipt and disbursement journals, balancing your checkbook each month should take only an hour or so. Put your checks in numerical order and check off checks that came back on your cash disbursements journal. Look for the coded amount that the bank entered during processing. If you or they made an error, you can catch it before your account becomes uncorrectable. Make a list of those checks that have not yet been processed and tally the amounts. Use the same procedure with your cash-receipts journal or the deposit column of your check journal, making sure that all deposits appear on the bank statement. If a deposit doesn't appear, it is probably still in transit and should appear on the next statement. Starting with the balance that appears on the statement, add any deposits in transit and subtract the total outstanding checks. That will give you a book balance that should match your own records. Then adjust your balance for any bank charges. As your business grows, other factors that will affect your bookkeeping include:

Cash versus Accrual: The approach described above is a cash-base bookkeeping system, reflecting expenditures made and funds actually received. An accrual-based system reflects anticipated income and expenses. That is, if you billed 10 people for $100 each, during a month, and only seven have paid, the other three billings are taken into account. This system requires the maintenance of a sales journal, in which you enter the date, name, amount, and product or service for each invoice. This might have distribution columns for different types of sales (retainer, project fees, etc.). This is used to create an accounts-receivable account. This approach more truly represents your business activity during a month. The cash-based system shows only what you have received, not what you have earned. Counter-balancing a sales journal is a purchase journal or ledger indicating debts incurred during a month. Consultants, however, are unlikely to have a great backlog of unpaid bills to keep track of unless activity is very high.

General ledger: The general ledger is a summary of the other journals. Each page lists the accounts or column headings recorded in the other journals. Large companies maintain a general ledger on a monthly basis, but you can sum up your financial picture quarterly. The general ledger is the basis for quarterly financial reports.

Financial statements: A financial statement is a report on your finances during a period of time. There are three types of financial statements, including the balance sheet, which sums up assets (cash, billings, property) and all liabilities or debts, leaving you with the net worth of the business. Profit-and-loss, or income, statements start with a record of all money received—your gross income. Consultants are not likely to encounter any returns or allowances unless dealing with a physical product, such as books. These returns or allowances are discounted to give you a net-income figure. This is reduced by direct cost. Direct costs are more typical of manufacturing and retail than of a service, but you may have expenses that fit into this category, such as subcontracted work, printing expenses for a book, or anything that relates directly to a specific project. A graphic artist or photographer is more likely to have direct costs than a business-management consultant. Deducting these costs from net income yields the business's gross profit. Deduct normal business expenses, including rent, utilities, travel, and office supplies, from the gross profit to find the net operating profit or loss. This process closely resembles the three basic sections of the tax forms for sole proprietors (Schedule C-Form 1040), for partnerships (Form

1065), and for corporations (Form 1120 or 1120S). These forms divide into income, cost of goods sold, and deductions.

A statement of financial position shows where money is coming from and how it is being spent over a period of time. Tally assets and liabilities at the beginning and end of the period to find the net increase or decrease in funds. It can be particularly helpful in planning for major expenditures.

Annual Budget: During the first two or three years of business it can be difficult to prepare an annual budget because growth and change occur so rapidly. Basically, the annual budget forecasts your income and expenses over the coming year or years. At the beginning of each calendar or fiscal year, analyze the sources of income and the expenditures of the previous year, adjust them according to anticipated growth, inflation, and obligations. If you anticipate accurately, the figures can help you make important decisions or recognize problems. For instance, you might project an income growth from $20,000 to $28,000 based on a growing number of retainer fees and longer billing time. You also might have decided to hire some office help, but don't know how much you can afford for it. The budget can help you analyze the relationship between increased income and increased expenses. How much of that $8,000 will go to added publicity costs, travel, telephone and office expenses? If you spend your money on paying a salary to a secretary, it may put you in a lower tax bracket. How much do you spend on secretarial services now? Must you have someone available everyday, or should you continue to use outside services? A well-prepared budget can help you answer these questions.

One danger of doing your own bookkeeping is that you may be unaware of IRS rules and regulations regarding acceptable expenses, reporting requirements, tax payment schedules, and the like. The IRS publishes several useful guides, but it takes patience and prior knowledge to understand the IRS's bureaucratese. For example, depending on your form of business, you might be able to deduct a bad check under the category of bad debts. But you would not be allowed to take the deduction if the bill wasn't paid at all. To exacerbate problems with the IRS, consultants are likely to have businesses in their homes, expense accounts, and irregular income, and as such, are most likely to be audited.

Some difficult tax areas and some suggestions on record keeping that may help you avoid trouble follow. This list is not comprehensive! Each business has its own pecularities.

Petty Cash: Consultants tyically have many out-of-pocket expenses, which are valid and deductible, but very difficult to document. Establish a petty cash fund of $10 to $100 depending on your needs. Use this for cash expenses and balance your receipts against the remaining cash at the end of each week or month. Another system is to bill your business account for out-of-pocket expenses, documenting the expenses with receipts and/or an explanation of how the money was spent.

Travel expenses: If you travel extensively, buy expense journals and document expenditures as you travel. Use business checks, credit cards, or petty cash, or bill your business at the end of the trip.

Transportation expenses: The IRS differentiates these from travel expenses. Transportation concerns fares and the use of your car. Most consultants use their cars for both personal and business purposes, and there are two ways of deducting the costs as a business expense. In both cases, keep track of mileage for business purposes. Note it in your calendar, with destination and purpose, or buy a journal from a stationer and keep it in your glove compartment. The easiest method is to take the current mileage allowance as a deduction. As of 1981, the government allows 21¢ per mile. You probably can take a larger deduction if you use a percentage system, in which you need records of expenses for operating and maintaining your car. This system allows for depreciation, and a specific formula is used. Figure what percentage of the year's total mileage was for business and take the proportionate amount of all expenses as a business deduction.

Entertainment: Document the business purpose of entertainment. Detail with whom you had dinner, what was discussed, and how it related to business.

Education: You can deduct courses and seminars that improve your business or professional skills, but not for those that prepare you to enter the field. For example, if you have no training in photography and want to become a photographer, you cannot deduct photography courses. If, on the other hand, you are a photographer and take a course in some specialized area, such as color development or camera repair, you can deduct the tuition.

Business in your home: If you use a room exclusively for business, you can deduct part of your rent or mortgage and utilities as an expense. The percentage can be figured on the basis of square footage or on the total number of rooms.

Payroll: You are required to deduct taxes for employees, according to their income and number of dependents. You are also required to pay social security and deduct your employees' part of the social security payment. If you do not submit payment of funds withheld for social security, federal and withholding taxes, you commit a felony. If you have employees, you should have a reliable bookkeeper. If you are incorported and draw a salary you are an employee.

Consultant's fees and sub-contractors: If you pay $600 or more in a year to someone for consulting or contracted services, you must submit Form 1099.

Self-employment tax: Sole proprietors and unincorporated partners with net earning of $400 or more must file a Schedule SE Form 1040 with their income taxes. For 1981, the rate was 8.1% of the net operating profit.

Quarterly Taxes: Whether or not you are incorporated, the government expects you to pay estimated quarterly taxes on the 15th day of the fourth, sixth, and ninth months and on the 15th day of the first month after the close of the tax year. These tax payments are based on the anticipated operating profit for the current tax year or the actual operating profit for the preceding year. Your accountant will advise you as to which is applicable. If you don't pay by that date, the unpaid portion is subject to a fine unless your payments equal those made for the same quarters of the previous year.

The IRS's Tax Guide for Small Businesses contains 192 pages of fine print and refers to dozens of other IRS publications for aspects of record keeping and reporting. Rather than wade through these publications, hire an accountant to help you prepare your taxes, to advise you on developing your business, and to enable you to keep as much money as possible out of the government's hands.

You and Your Accountant

An accountant is key in developing a business. Like your lawyer, he constitutes a critical member of your planning team, and you may want to make your accountant a director of your corporation, if your state requires more than one director.

You can find an accountant through your contact network. Ask consultants in work similar to yours and ask your lawyer whose accounting help they find satisfactory. Your lawyer and your accountant must show mutual respect and must be able to work together.

An accountant is best used as a business planner and adviser on business and personal taxes. He is not best used as a bookkeeper, mainly because he will charge high fees for such work.

Your accountant must know as much as you do about your business plans, projected revenues, and method of operating. Give him this information in a precise, economical, thoughtful format. Don't spew papers at your accountant and expect him to decipher them.

If, for example, you have operated as a sole proprietor and wish to incorporate, discuss the matter with your accountant beforehand. Discuss the details of your business, including how much you make, how much you spend, what is profitable to you, what isn't, what you project for the next six months, or the next year, and how you foresee your business to take you to that accomplishment.

Given this information, an accountant can suggest what you should do to realize your desires.

Meet with your accountant regularly, perhaps each quarter, taking his advice on how often you should meet. Discuss your cash flow, pension plans, tax shelters, investments, borrowing capital, salary, and taxes. An accountant cannot help in any of these areas if you meet with him only once a year at the conclusion of your fiscal year.

At the beginning of your relationship, ask your accountant to list the categories you should bring up for regular review. With this list, you can be assured that major areas will be covered regularly.

You need only a few hours a year with your accountant. However, you will be in touch on a regular basis through your bookkeeper. It is, then, important that your bookkeeper and accountant have a good relationship.

CONCLUSION

If you follow the suggestions in this book, you can achieve success. But be prepared for the demanding and uncertain life of a consultant. These suggestions will make your life easier and your success more likely:

- Add people to your contact network; a consultant cannot succeed without one.
- Develop your service line, adding services that are logical extensions of your first undertaking.
- Diversify your sources of income. Consultants who rely only on billable hours for revenue considerably limit their potential income and face possible early burn-out.
- Promote yourself; use the media to achieve third-party recognition as an acknowledged expert in your field.
- Learn to negotiate. Don't undersell yourself, but develop contracts that are mutually acceptable.
- Subcontract; find sub-contractors through your contact network and use them to enhance your potential earnings.
- Follow up on leads; do not allow opportunities to go untapped, and make sure that all leads are followed through to the end of their usefulness.
- Rely on experts, including a lawyer, an accountant, and a bookkeeper. They will teach you to improve your business.
- Develop limits. As a consultant you can work 24 hours a day if you want to. But don't do it. You must be refreshed and confident. Take time out for yourself.
- Don't give up. Success is achieved through a relentless determination to succeed and a willingness to do whatever is necessary to succeed.
- Keep your sense of humor. Living well is the best revenge.

Good luck!

SAMPLES SECTION: TABLE OF CONTENTS

Potential Client Log Sheet

Potential Client Name:

Position or Title:

Company:

Address:

Telephone:

Contact (when and where met):

Contact Through (person who introduced you):

Notes:

Record of Communications

Date	**Synopsis of Conversation**	**Follow-up**

Contact and Marketing Letters

General points to remember when composing the following letters:

- Type these letters on your stationery.
- Include your telephone number.
- Keep copies.

Essentials of a Contact Follow-Up Letter

- Send this letter within 48 hours of meeting the contact.

- Use an informal, friendly tone.

- Express your pleasure in the meeting in the first paragraph, making sure to mention the place and circumstances.

- Mention in the second paragraph ideas that arose during your conversation that you are interested in pursuing.

- Indicate why you are interested, mentioning work you have done or are doing which may have a bearing on the topic.

- Third paragraph suggests a possible follow-up. If you propose a meeting, call within 10 days to schedule it.

- Enclose pertinent materials.

Sample New Contact Follow-Up Letter

Ms. Claire Smith, President
Boston Children's Home, Inc.
365 Huntington Avenue
Boston, MA 02111

Dear Ms. Smith:

It was nice to meet you last night at the Calvert's cocktail party. I'm so glad I had the opportunity to learn about the current projects of the Boston Children's Home. I knew, of course, about the fine reputation of the Home. Now I know why that reputation exists!

As I mentioned last night, I've been working with many human service agencies by assisting them to strengthen their boards of directors. As you know, one of my clients is your friend Peter Robbins of the Family Service Agency.

Given what you said about your plans for the Board of the Home, it might be advantageous for us to meet again and see if there's a chance we might work together. I'm enclosing our brochure and a recent article from the *Winchester Star* about our work with a client in that community. I think you might like to see them.

I'll call you next week to see about setting up a meeting. In the meantime, please send me a brochure about the agency. I'd enjoy having the oportunity to review it.

With thanks,

Sincerely,

Consultant

Essentials of a Letter to be Sent to Contacts Upon Leaving Regular Employment to Establish a Consultancy

- Have this letter printed on your stationery.
- Allow room to type an inside address and salutation.
- Mention in the first paragraph that you are leaving the XYZ company to establish an independent practice. Suggest why your experience in this position qualifies you to start a business.
- Don't mention it if you have been fired from your position. Indicate that the timing and reason for leaving were entirely your own.
- Mention in the second paragraph the services you offer. Be specific, but do not include too many details.
- Detail the intended follow-up in the third paragraph. Is it worth calling the contact? If he could be a key person in your network, a call is a good idea.
- Note the date of the call on your calendar. The date should be 10 business days after the date of your letter.
- Enclose descriptive materials about your business.
- Write a one- to two-line personal note at the foot of the letter.

May 20, 1981

Mr. Joe Lewis, Coordinator
Special Education Program
Somerville Public Schools
345 Highland Avenue
Somerville, Mass. 02141

Dear Joe:

As Chairman of the Special Education Department of Cambridge High School, I've often had occasion to work with you over the years. Because I've enjoyed our association, I want you to know that I'm leaving my position at the end of this semester to establish a consulting business. My practice will deal with contemporary educational issues, particularly problems faced by displaced educators and by school systems reducing the work force.

My business will center on two primary areas:

- I will provide services to the teachers who by choice or because of a forced layoff are leaving teaching and looking for jobs in the public and private sectors. I will provide private counseling, identify resources and positions, largely in the Boston area, and offer workshops to small groups of educators to prepare them for the job market.

- I will act as a consultant to school systems that must implement reductions in their work forces. I will act as an adviser in all aspects of policy conception and implementation.

I am enclosing an article from the *Cambridge Chronicle* in which I discuss some of the options available to teachers leaving public education. The article suggests some services that I will provide.

I would like to discuss in greater detail my service line and will call you within 10 business days to make an appointment.

It would be my pleasure to work with you as I develop this new, timely enterprise.

Sincerely,

Consultant

Essentials of the Sophisticated Fan Letter

- Keep a professional tone.
- Present a specific compliment in the first paragraph. Refer to a recent piece of work or achievement.
- Indicate in the second paragraph what you are doing that may interest the star. Indicate that you are a peer so that the person to whom you are writing will want you as part of his network.
- Indicate whether you have any work that may be of particular interest. If you can supply a piece of helpful information, do so.
- Suggest a meeting in the third paragraph. Don't be too pushy. You are a colleague, not just a fan; project interest, not haste.
- Enclose materials that may interest the leader, but don't overdo it.

Sophisticated Fan Letter Sample

Mr. Brian O'Connell, President
Independent Sector, Inc.
1010 New Hampshire Ave., N.W.
Washington, D.C.20036

Dear Mr. Connell:

I read with interest your remarks in this morning's *New York Times*. Your advocacy of H.R. 501, allowing taxpayers who use the short income tax form to itemize their charitable contributions, seems most worthy, and I wish you well with your efforts. I will send a letter about the matter to my congressman, Joe Doaks.

Given your strenuous support of the voluntary principle and of measures to bolster nonprofit organizations, you may be interested to learn about my work with such groups. I am a consultant providing technical assistance to public charities and tax-exempt organizations, especially in the areas of fund raising and organizational development. I enclose my brochure for your convenience.

It would be most helpful to me to hear in greater detail about your work and that of Independent Sector, Inc. As I travel to Washington from time to time, perhaps it would be convenient for us to meet. In the meantime, I shall urge my clients to send letters recommending H.R. 501 to their congressmen.

With all good wishes,

Sincerely,

Consultant

Essentials of a Congratulatory Note

- Type or write this note, depending on how well you know the recipient and how legible your handwriting is.
- Send this note to people you already know.
- Use a formal or informal tone.
- Compliment the individual, naming his achievement first.
- Cite the source of your knowledge, especially if your source was the media.
- Enclose articles containing the announcement of the achievement. People always need extra copies of such clips.
- If there is a connection between the achievement and you, or you belong to the organization making the award, mention it.
- Indicate when and where you want to meet with the individual.

Congratulatory Note Sample

Mr. Hubert Jessup, Moderator
WHDH Radio Talk Show
441 Stuart St.
Boston, MA 02116

Dear Hubert,

Congratulations on your appointment as moderator of the WHDH Radio Talk Show. I read about it in today's *Globe* and hasten to send my best wishes. What a splendid appointment for you, and what a boost to the city's evening talk circuit!

I'd very much enjoy seeing you again soon and hearing the inside story of your appointment. In the meantime, I'll enjoy listening to you on the air.

With all good wishes,

Sincerely,

Friend

Essentials of the Update Note

- This note keeps your contacts updated on your activities.
- Send one when you introduce a new service, publish an article that is of interest, or want to report something notable.
- Type this note.
- Use an informal, professional tone.
- Get to the point in the first paragraph.
- If you intend to follow up, indicate in the second paragraph how you will do so and when.
- Conclude by indicating that you hope that the recipient's business is going well.
- Enclose relevant materials.

Sample Update Note

Mr. Robert Dobson, Executive Director
Innercity Human Resources, Inc.
501 Washington St.
Baltimore, Maryland 21212

Dear Mr. Dobson:

You may remember our meeting last fall during which we discussed your organization's need for marketing and public relations assistance.

I want to inform you that our firm has a new associate, Grace Peters, who is an expert in the field.

Grace has expertise in assisting nonprofit organizations to create effective mass-market documents. She has worked with such organizations as the Big Brothers of Tacoma, the Cleveland Symphony, and Project Resolve in Baltimore.

I'd like to have Grace call you next week to discuss your needs in detail.

By the way, I saw an article about Innercity Human Resource in *The Tab* last week. I was glad to see that one of the programs we discussed has now developed to such an extent.

With thanks,

Sincerely,

Consultant

Essentials of a Letter to Individuals Connected to You

Through a Professional Association or Club

- Have this letter offset printed on your stationery; do not xerox it.
- Allow space to type an inside address and salutation.
- Use a professional, fraternal tone.
- Mention in the first paragraph your connection with the individual.
- Mention in the second paragraph your services.
- Indicate any intended follow-up in the third paragraph.
- Enclose pertinent materials.

Sample Colleague Letter

Mr. Edward Chavers, President
American Metal Corp., Inc.
One Cityhill Drive
Toledo, Ohio 20617

Dear Ed,

As you know, I've recently joined the local Kiwanis and am very glad I did so. Everyone has been most kind and helpful. One thing that I've been asked about is my business. I've decided to send the members some information for their files.

I set up my management consulting business two years ago. My associates and I primarily offer technical assistance to new profit and nonprofit businesses. Our primary activities include bookkeeping, accounting, developing long-range plans, performing market development and projection, creating advertising strategies, and maximizing profit potential.

The enclosed brochure provides greater detail about our work, as does the enclosed article from the *Daily Blade*, which was interested in running a piece about our work with small businesses.

If I can provide further information, let me know. I look forward to seeing you at our Wednesday lunches, and I'd be happy to drop by and discuss our work with you at your convenience, if you ever need our services.

Sincerely,

Consultant

Essentials of a Mini-Case

Consulting firms use mini-cases regularly as sales tools in approaching new clients, in defining expertise, and in evidencing a good track record. Mini-cases are often included in proposals but may also be used as a leave-behind or to create a portfolio of experience.

- Print each case separately on your stationery.
- Use a highly professional and more formal tone than that used in other publicity materials.
- Cite the client's name if possible or the project's title.
- Indicate the reasons why the project was carried out.
- Cite the project's scope, its results, its benefits to the client, and the techniques used.
- Indicate how this experience can benefit potential clients.

Mini-Case

Long-Range Forecasting Properties of State-of-the-Art

Models of Demand for Electric Energy

Radical changes in energy markets in recent years and the expectation of continuing change as new technologies and energy-use patterns develop have contributed to a growing interest among planners, forecasters, and policy makers in improved methods of analyzing and forecasting the demand for electricity. Mathematical modeling approaches have attracted particular attention.

The Power Institute of America (PIA), as the electric power industry's principal sponsor of research and development (and sponsor of this study), is concerned with developing and applying improved methods of forecasting and analyzing energy demand, especially the demand for electricity.

Forecasts' study assessed the state of the art of electricity demand and load forecasting models. Our study focused on eight models potentially useful for long-range electricity-use forecasting. All published econometric models were reviewed for compilation of an annotated bibliography. A major objective was to alert PIA to the forecasting implications of these model features and to formulate suggestions concerning the most promising lines of development for improvements in the state of the art.

During its research, Forecasts has built what is almost certainly the most complete data base for electricty-demand forecasting outside of the utility industry.

Essentials of a Project Listing

(Note: Some consultants, especially those who are consulting while they still have a regular job, use project listings as leave-behinds or as part of a proposal. Print them in small quantities on your stationery.)

- Divide the project descriptions according to the different aspects of your service line.
- Cite clients and, if appropriate, associates.
- Describe the unique characteristics of each project, emphasizing the client's needs and the consultant's skills.

Sample Project Listing

Audiovisual Scripts

Chomerics Materials, Inc., produced by Envision Corp.

Chomerics, a specialist in dispersion chemistry, produces gaskets, sealants, laminates, and other materials for high-reliability electronic systems. This sales show compares Chomeric's products to those of its competitors, emphasizing technological advancements and laboratory facilities.

M&T Chemicals, Inc., produced by Envision Corp.

M&T is a $250-million international corporation specializing in tin-based chemicals. The portrait, used primarily to introduce potential customers and new employees to the overall operation, covers the company's history, range of products and their applications, research facilities, and customer services.

Charles Stark Draper Laboratory, produced by Envision Corp.

Draper Laboratory is a nonprofit research-and-development organization best known for its work in aeronautics and aviation. The documentary-style, multi-media show highlights the laboratory's accomplishments and atmosphere and the process of developing and applying new technologies. The show is used for recruitment, tours, and presentations to potential research sponsors.

Data General, produced by Envision Corp.

This slide show is used by sales personnel to introduce Data General Corp.'s line of small-business computers. It focuses on the products' operational characteristics, capabilities, and growth potential.

Journalism

"Vickery Talks on Future," *Cambridge Chronicle*, October 2, 1980. David Vickery, assistant city manager for community development, presents the Cambridge approach at the International Conference on Urban Design.

"The Design Riddle," *Boston Monthly*, September, 1980. Editorial musings on the relationship between art, design, and urban planning for the publication's special issue on design.

Essentials of a Service-Line Synopsis

- Offset-print the synopsis on your stationery.
- Make the synopsis no longer than one page.
- Use a positive, professional tone.
- Mention why and by whom services are needed.
- Mention the service-providers' qualifications.
- Itemize services so that they can be read at a glance.

Service-Line Synopsis

Jane Doe and Associates
Special Events Planning

A special event is a rare occasion and usually one of great importance. Few organizations have the extra staff needed to organize and perform the myriad details involved in staging a special event. Jane Doe, former director of event planning at AXC Advertising, can help create a 1000-personnel conference or a 20-person dinner party that will run smoothly and efficiently. Jane Doe and Associates can help your group develop an exciting program with a realistic budget and ensure that services are provided as you planned. Why burden your staff with extra work and run the risk of disaster? Expert experience can assure the success of your special event. Jane Doe and Associates' services include: program planning, invitations and returns, site selection, catering, displays and decoration, awards and memorabilia, audiovisual programs, entertainment, brochures, menus, printed materials, and photographers.

Essentials of a Brochure

- Use a neat, professional design, typesetting, and printing.
- Create a self-mailer by folding an 8½- x 11-in. sheet in thirds.
- Use a confident, light, and professional tone, and be brief.
- Focus on the client's need rather than on yours. Use an "other-directed" style, which means consider your audience and write for it.
- Include your business name, address, and telephone number on the front panel, plus a three- or four-word description of your service line.
- The other outside panel should be designed like an envelope, with your business name and return address. Its design should be consistent with your stationery and cards.
- Describe in the first inner panel the nature of your business, your clients, and how your services are performed. You can also include some brief historical information on the business.
- Use the remaining inner panels to itemize your service line. Include as many selling points as possible, explaining why particular services are needed and how the service can benefit them. Avoid negative comparisons with other services.
- Present philosophical statements and citations of experience after service descriptions.
- Cite secondary or supporting services.
- Feature in the in-fold panel biographies of the principal and his associates. Do not include biographies of associates who are not in regular employ unless you are sure they will be working with you for an extended time.
- Cite in the principal's biography education, awards, teaching experience, and other qualifications, such as prior experience and authorship.
- If you have room and you have prestigious clients, include a partial listing of them.

Partial Sample Brochure

Jeffrey Lant Associates

Fundraising

and

Organizational

Development

1558 MASSACHUSETTS AVENUE, SUITE 33
CAMBRIDGE, MASSACHUSETTS 02138
Telephone: 617-547-6372
(Answering Service) 617-661-2622

Jeffrey Lant Associates

1558 MASSACHUSETTS AVENUE, SUITE 33
CAMBRIDGE, MASSACHUSETTS 02138

STAFF AND CONSULTING ASSOCIATES

Jeffrey L. Lant. Dr. Lant received a B.A. degree *summa cum laude* in history and political science from the University of California, Santa Barbara, and M.A. and Ph.D. degrees in history from Harvard, where he was a Woodrow Wilson Fellow, Harvard Prize Fellow, and winner of a Harvard College Master's Award. Dr. Lant has been an administrator at Boston College and Harvard University. He is the author of many articles on a wide variety of subjects and one volume of history. He has lectured widely and has taught at Harvard, Boston College, and Northeastern University.

CONSULTING ASSOCIATES

Jeffrey Lant Associates draws on a wide range of expert consultants in diverse areas. Part of the function of Jeffrey Lant Associates is to provide both non-profit and profit-making organizations with the kinds of talent they need when they need it. These consultants include educators, lawyers, accountants, financial experts, architects, graphic designers, copy editors, media specialists, marketing personnel and administrative talent.

111

- Have the brochure designed as a self-mailer.
- Have it printed on legal-sized paper divided into four sections on each side.
- Include the following panels on side 1:
    1. A registration form containing space for registrants' names, addresses, and telephone numbers.
    2. An explanation of the workshop, who should attend, and who will conduct it.
    3. Information on special features.
    4. A complete outline of the workshop topics.
- Include the following panels on side 2:
    1. Information on cancellation, refunds, possible tax deductibility, and a telephone number for further information.
    2. A map of the workshop site or directions from nearby communities.
    3. A mailing panel.
    4. A cover with the name of the workshop, date, time, location, and sponsor names.
- A sponsoring institution generally provides all material for the brochure except for panels 2 to 4 on side one. Samples of these panels follow.
- Submit a photograph.

Partial Workshop Brochure

NONPROFIT ORGANIZATION DEVELOPMENT TRAINING WORKSHOP:
For Improving Development Skills and Fund Raising Techniques:

What Is the Development Training Workshop?

The Development Training Workshop is a day-long intensive training program, moderately priced to enable maximum attendance by nonprofit personnel. The emphasis is on developing individual skills and on gaining insight into the difficult process of grantsmanship and development. Participants can expect to obtain immediately usable information as well as general training in development theory and practice.

Who Should Attend the Development Training Workshop?

All those associated with nonprofit organizations, particularly executive directors, trustees, and development personnel. All those who are, or will be, responsible for development and fund-raising campaigns.

Workshop Leader:

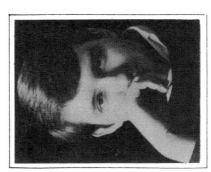

The Development Training Workshop will be presented by Jeffrey L. Lant, Ph.D., president of Jeffrey Lant Associates, Inc., a management and development firm for nonprofit organizations. He received his M.A. and Ph.D. degrees from Harvard University, where he was a Woodrow Wilson Fellow, Harvard Prize Fellow and winner of a Harvard College Master's Award. Before forming his firm, Dr. Lant taught and/or administered at Harvard University, Boston College and Northeastern University. Dr. Lant is included in "Who's Who in the East" and "The

Dictionary of International Biography." He is the author of **DEVELOPMENT TODAY: A GUIDE FOR NONPROFIT ORGANIZATIONS** and is the editor of a forthcoming volume on Harvard.

Special Features:

Each participant in the Workshop will receive, as part of the registration cost, a copy of **DEVELOPMENT TODAY: A GUIDE FOR NONPROFIT ORGANIZATIONS** by Jeffrey L. Lant. **DEVELOPMENT TODAY** is an essential 200 page guide for nonprofit organizations. It includes detailed information on all workshop topics as well as 40 pages of sample documents you can use. **DEVELOPMENT TODAY** regularly sells for $24.95 and is available direct from Jeffrey Lant Associates, Inc. at 50 Follen Street, #507, Cambridge, Ma. 02138.

Program Outline:

1. An Introduction to Development
 a) Basic Reference Tools
 b) Information Up-Date Services
 c) Federal Funding Opportunities

2. Some Candid Thoughts About Fund Raising In the 80s
 a) What the books never tell you
 b) Fund raising is not objective
 c) There's not as much money as you think
 d) How to get what there is

3. Beginning the Development Process
 a) Toward a Development Philosophy
 b) The Strategy of Development
 c) Who Should Participate
 d) Developing Goals and Needs Priorities
 e) What you need to know before asking for money
 f) The Consultant's Role

4. The Executive Director
 a) Crucial to the Development Process
 b) How much time will it take
 c) How to balance development with other duties
 d) Developing a Controlled Process

5. The Board of Directors
 a) The Chairman's Role
 b) How to find a chairman who'll work
 c) Who should be a member of the Board
 d) If the Board has not done development work
 e) If the Board will not do development work
 f) The Board's responsibility

6. Establishing the Contact Network
 a) Why Development efforts fail without one
 b) What to know about yourself, your Board, your organization
 c) How to find out

7. The Proposal
 a) How to develop successful proposals
 b) Proposal modules
 c) Proposal structure
 d) Proposal language
 e) Cutting and pasting
 d) What to do when you know
 e) Encountering resistance
 f) Writing the Campaign Document
 g) Keeping control

8. The Narrative
 a) Beginning with an eye-catcher
 b) Organizational History and Background
 c) Placing an Organization in context
 d) Gathering persuasive evidence
 e) Using Testimonials
 f) Financial Information
 g) Making the Proposal

9. The Budget
 a) How much to ask for
 b) Budgeting for alternatives
 c) Negotiating
 d) Narrative budgets
 e) Line-item budgets
 f) Ask for what you really need
 g) Direct/indirect costs

10. The Proposal Package
 a) The cover letter
 b) Title page and introduction
 c) Table of contents
 d) Attention getting devices
 e) Reader notes
 f) Appendices
 g) Required forms and documents

11. The Interview
 a) How to get an appointment with someone who matters
 b) How to prepare for it
 c) What to look like
 d) What to say
 e) Note taking

12. Getting Turned Down
 a) How to respond to a "No"
 b) Building toward a "Yes"
 c) Persistence pays off
 d) Making friends

13. What To Do When It's "Yes"
 a) The Process isn't over
 b) Why Organizations fail at this point
 c) Securing your position
 d) The benefit of courtesy

14. Building For The Next Grant
 a) The Development Process Never Ends
 b) Some tips on project management
 c) Keeping your connections
 d) The process of renewing
 e) Promoting your organization
 f) Acting like a winner

113

Essentials of a Query Letter to an Editor
with Whom You Are Connected

- Use a formal or informal tone depending on the strength of your connection.
- Mention your connection in the first paragraph.
- Present your ideas in the second paragraph, giving an outline of the article, suggesting who would read it and why it is timely.
- Mention, rather than stress, your qualifications for writing the article in the third paragraph. The more familiar your contact is with you and your work, the less stress you should place on qualifications.
- Suggest a length, deadline date, graphics, and possible payment for the article in the next paragraph.
- Conclude by suggesting possible follow-up, stating, for example, that you will call within 10 business days.

Sample Letter to an Editor with Whom You are Connected

Mr. Christian Smallwood, Editor
Business Section
Christian Science Monitor
One Norway Street
Boston, MA 02115

Dear Chris,

I haven't been in touch for a while, but I am sending an idea that I hope will be of interest.

There are, as you may know, more than 500,000 nonprofit organizations in the U.S., including schools, colleges, hospitals, and community-service organizations. They are essential to our society.

Unfortunately, President Reagan's budget cutbacks imperil the survival of many of these groups, particularly those in the human services.

I'd like to submit a column for the Business Section suggesting some practical steps these groups can take to improve their chances of surviving. I think this section of the paper is best for my article because the organizations I will write about are nonprofit corporations.

I'd like to submit about 750 words by next Thursday, April 17th, and I hope to receive $150 in payment.

I'll call next week to see if the idea appeals to you and if the timing is convenient.

With thanks,

Sincerely,

Friend

Essentials of a Query Letter to an
Editor with Whom You Are Not Connected

- Address this letter to a specific individual. Call the publication to get the correct spelling of the editor's name, his position, and his address. Do not write a "to-whom-it-may-concern" letter.

- Use a professional, forthright tone.

- Present an idea in the first paragraph and give the flavor of the article, suggesting why it is timely. Do not assume that an editor will know about the matter you suggest, but do not be condescending.

- Present in the second paragraph the reasons that you are the best person to write this article, stating, for example, that you are a recognized expert.

- Outline the particulars, including length, due date, a description of graphics, and possible payment in the third paragraph.

- Conclude by suggesting possible follow-up, stating, for example, that you will call within 10 business days.

Sample Query Letter to an

Editor with Whom You Are Not Connected

Mr. Robert Garwood, Editor
Business Section
The New York Times
10 42nd Street
New York, New York 10028

Dear Mr. Garwood:

Many of the more than 500,000 nonprofit organizations in the nation face difficult times in this decade. They are being hard-hit by President Reagan's proposed federal budget cuts, inflation, the decline in real dollars donated by America's 22,000 private foundations, and the decline in the number of Americans making charitable gifts.

Yet nonprofit organizations, including schools, universities, hospitals, and community groups, are essential to our way of life.

I'm the president of a Cambridge, Mass. consulting firm specializing in providing technical assistance to nonprofit organization particularly in the fund-raising and management areas. My clients include many small, community-based agencies that are being particularly affected.

I'd like to submit for your consideration a 750-word column detailing some practical, inexpensive steps that these groups can take to help themselves survive in this decade. I can send this article to you, ready for publication, within two weeks. I hope to receive $250 in payment.

I shall call you within 10 business days to discuss my idea and the particulars surrounding publication. I look forward to speaking with you.

Sincerely,

Consultant

Essentials of an Article by You

- Type your article double-spaced with about 250 words per page.
- Suggest a headline that describes your main point, but the publication is likely to select its own headline.
- Promote your business by writing in such a way that your article could become a leave-behind.
- Include a tag line at the end, indicating the name of your business, its location and the source of your expertise.
- Send the article with a brief cover letter suggesting the follow-up, stating, for example, that you will call within 10 business days to check your article's progress.

Tough times ahead for non profits not ready to fight

By DR. JEFFREY L. LANT

Over the next decade, many of the nation's 500,000 nonprofit organizations will face very difficult times. Because all of us are in some way touched by the work of these groups — through hospitals, universities, religious institutions, museums, human service agencies — what is happening ought to be of widespread concern.

To begin with, certain external factors are adversely affecting nonprofit organizations:

● Inflation. The major concern of every citizen is also first on the list of problems for nonprofit groups. Whether a nonprofit organization has an endowment or not, inflation is the enemy. Organizations without endowments are finding it more and more difficult to do business, particularly if they are agencies dealing with the needy and have relied upon any kind of user fees.

On the other hand, agencies with endowments are also having problems. The return on their capital investments, largely in stocks and bonds, has not been good in recent years. More and more, I hear of such organizations dipping into their capital to make good the difference between what they must have to operate and what they receive in revenue. The long term implications of this situation are most alarming.

This same inflation, with the weakness it has brought to the stock and bond markets, is also wreaking havoc with the assets of foundations, which have traditionally supplied nonprofit organizations with grants. The Ford Foundation, the nation's premier grantsmaking foundation, provides a clear example of what is happening: its assets have been steadily shrinking over the last decade and thus its ability to make grants — at the very time inflation has soared and undercut the value of all those dollars still being given. Nearly every one of the nation's 28,000 private foundations finds itself in the same situation.

● Budget and Tax Cutting Initiatives. President Reagan says he will take $20 billion off the federal budget. He also says the defense establishment will be dramatically improved. These two presidential objectives spell trouble for nonprofit organizations, particularly those in the human services and education. The cutback in federal funds will have two important effects. Organizations relying on these dollars will face the likelihood of cutting back on the programs and personnel supported by these dollars. They will also lose that percentage of the grant termed "overhead," which goes to support their fixed operating expenses. In fact, these overhead monies have constituted a necessary source of unrestricted funds to many organizations.

Local tax cutting initiatives are adding to the problems of nonprofit organizations. Not only will local authorities be unable to contract out for as many of the services provided by nonprofit organizations (a fact which the Boston Shakespeare Company discovered the day after the election when one of its school contracts was cancelled); also, local foundations will feel pressured to support projects previously funded by state dollars.

The Committee of the Permanent Charity Fund, Boston's bellwether foundation, gave this excuse after its December meeting to dozens of local nonprofit organizations which had applied for funds. Many of these organizations are now in dire straits and several will close in the current year.

● Corporate Support. Many people in the nonprofit world took heart last year when for the first time in American history corporate philanthropy outpaced foundation giving. I was not among them. The monies that corpo-

(617) 547-6372
50 FOLLEN STREET, SUITE 507 • CAMBRIDGE, MASSACHUSETTS 02138

rations give are almost always donated to very conservative, established projects such as art museums, opera companies, public television extravaganzas. They are safe, non-controversial and have immediate public relations benefits. Corporations have never been among the philanthropic pacesetters, and, in this conservative decade, they are not going to change their habits.

Adding to the problems of nonprofit organizations are certain internal difficulties. Unlike the external problems, these difficulties can be dealt with — and must be, if the organization stands any chance of surviving the years ahead.

● Marketing Problems. Nonprofit organizations do not, on the whole, understand marketing. Organizations are plagued by a lack of clarity about what they are in business to do, what it costs them to do it, and what their competition, both profit and not-for-profit, is doing.

Moreover, nonprofit organizations are too often unclear about the detailed needs of their service populations and now their proposed programs will solve community problems. Finally, organizations find it difficult to communicate this information to the public in a way which will be easily understood.

● Lack of Business Sense. Adding to the marketing difficulties, nonprofit organizations also suffer from a lack of business knowledge and from an inability to see that their services are amenable to business principles and are not at odds with them. Nearly all nonprofit organizations are also corporations under the law, not-for-profit corporations. Yet the executives of nonprofit organizations fail to see the connection between what they they do and what the executives of any other corporation must do to insure the success of their enterprise.

● Exclusively. Every nonprofit organization is begun by a dedicated group of people committed to some civic betterment. Yet, any organization succeeds only insofar as it brings others into the venture and enthuses them about the project. If the group remains exclusive, its chances of success are enormously reduced.

A commitment to broadening the base of the organization necessarily means building a strong, diverse board of directors. I have continually found that too many directors of nonprofit organizations are either ignorant of or unwilling to assume their obligations to govern.

Among their responsibilities perhaps the most misunderstood is a director's obligation either to give money or else work hard to find money for the organization. Unfortunately, executive directors are often unclear about how to motivate their boards to accept such responsibilities and how to attract worthy individuals to their organizations.

Serving on the board of a nonprofit organization should be regarded as a signal honor for any citizen — but it is a working honor, not a sinecure.

Sadly, thousands of nonprofit organizations around the country, dozens in Massachusetts, will go under in the next years. Many will take with them ideas which could have benefited all of us had their leaders done what was necessary to combat adverse circumstances and save their organizations. Fortunately, many other nonprofit organizations will make the necessary changes and will come through the difficult times ahead stronger than ever.

Jeffrey Lant is president of Jeffrey Lant Associates, Inc., a Cambridge firm supplying technical assistance to nonprofit organizations, and is the author of "Development Today: A Guide for Nonprofit Organizations."

Boston Herald American — Friday, February 6, 1981

Essentials of an Article about You

- Don't wait to be sought out; instead, think of a news angle.
- Use your network to find a link with the editor of the publication in which you wish the article to appear.
- If you can't find a link, propose the article yourself, following the format of the query letter to an individual with whom you are not connected.
- Newspapers and magazines will not publish purely self-promotional articles. Think of a general angle, such as what you are doing that is interesting, helpful, important, new, or unusual. If you can't think of an article from an editor's viewpoint, it probably won't get published.
- Make sure that the piece you conceive will promote your business when published. Unless it does so, it loses its primary value as a leave-behind.
- Follow up an initial letter to the editor within 10 business days.
- Don't be shy about getting an article about yourself published. It represents third-party validation and has real usefulness.

THE BOSTON GLOBE   FRIDAY, JULY 18, 1980

SMALL BUSINESS
By ANSON SMITH

Helping small fund raisers

If your favorite nonprofit organization is small and getting nowhere in its efforts to raise money, there are pros such as Jeffrey Lant, PhD, who may be able to help.

Lant, 33, formerly a fund-raising administrator at Harvard, now heads his own small company, Jeffrey Lant Associates of Cambridge, a year-old firm specializing in helping small non-profit organizations raise money.

Says Lant:

"Most of these small organizations go about their fund raising in self-defeating ways. They don't

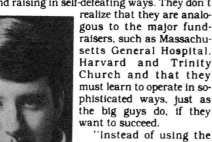

realize that they are analogous to the major fund-raisers, such as Massachusetts General Hospital, Harvard and Trinity Church and that they must learn to operate in sophisticated ways, just as the big guys do, if they want to succeed.

JEFFREY LANT

"Instead of using the big guys' methods, which rely on the who-knows-whom principle, small organizations typically develop a proposal. They go to one of the reference libraries and open books and they see that the Ford Foundation gives millions of dollars in their area and they write out a proposal and mail it off. And nothing happens. Usually, there is not even an acknowledgment."

Lant's company, consisting of himself and two assistants who also have academic backgrounds, begins its service to a client by sitting down with the organization's top people and helping them to make their short-term goals precise. Lant also asks clients to start thinking about their long-term goals.

The client is asked to answer such questions as, "Why do we exist?" and "What do we want to do specifically?"

Next, Lant and his staff draw up a series of documents, including a precise summary of the kinds of information every prospective giver must have: The background of the organization, for instance, specifics of the program the organization is engaged in and demonstrated successes of the organization.

"Then we begin to behave like the Harvards and the rest," says Lant. "We call monthly 'contact meetings' of the organization's directors and committed friends. At the first one we ask participants to fill out a form that has 30 questions designed to pinpoint people who can help the organization by using their influence." Lant says the questions include: Where do you bank? What insurance company or companies do you deal with? What stocks do you hold? Who do you know who works for a major corporation? What foundation contacts do you have, if any?

"We find that most people have more contacts, more clout, than they think," adds Lant. "We try to help them to use that clout so that the organization can reach its fund-raising goals."

Lant sits down with the executive director of the client organization and they put together an extensive memo cataloging all the contacts they have discovered as a result of the questionnaire. Later, these leads will be followed up by letter or telephone.

A second "contact' session" is held to widen the net. This time, 20 to 25 potential major donors are invited, and there are several speakers, including a 'star', who will give the main address and perhaps announce a large pledge to the organization.

"The first hour of the session is for drinking," Lant explains. "The second hour is for the presentation of the case for giving to the organization."

But no one puts the touch on at this meeting. Instead, all who were invited are sent follow-up letters politely soliciting their contributions. The letters are low-keyed. "We need your help," they say.

The pitch has been made.

The money starts rolling in.

Which is the name of the game.

(617) 547-6372
50 FOLLEN STREET, SUITE 507 • CAMBRIDGE, MASSACHUSETTS 02138

Essentials of a Press Release

- Have the release offset printed or use a high-quality photocopy.

- Use a professional, authoritative tone.

- Include the following information at or near the top of the release: the organization's or individual's name, address, and telephone number; the date of the release, the time when the release may be used (for example, "for immediate release"); the name of a contact person; and the names of individuals whose attention is being directed to the release.

- Include sufficient information to stimulate further attention from the media or to generate a short article.

- Use provocative quotations that establish the importance of the subject and your authority as an expert. Keep these quotations crisp.

- Follow up the press release with a telephone call within 10 business days, particularly if you wish to schedule media appearances.

- If possible, address the release to the attention of a specific individual.

MEDIA ADVISORY

For further information contact:
Mel Anderson
(303) 973-5127

Dr Jeffrey Lant
(617) 547-6372

August 15, 1982

"Jeffrey Lant provides the ultimate advice on giving advice!"

Cleveland Press

CONSULTING EXPERT TO TELL DENVER HOW TO CREATE JOBS, HELP ECONOMY

Dr Jeffrey Lant, author of THE CONSULTANT'S KIT: ESTABLISHING AND OPERATING YOUR SUCCESSFUL CONSULTING BUSINESS, will be in Denver on Tuesday, October 5 to promote his new best-seller and to advise residents how to cash in on one of America's growth fields -- consulting. On October 5, Lant will be available to the media for interviews. On Saturday, November 6 he will present his one-day intensive workshop "Establishing and Operating Your Successful Consulting Business."

Lant, who kicks off a seventeen state fall tour in September, is promoting his methods for creating lucrative part-time and full-time consulting jobs despite the flagging national economy. Lant will discuss:

- the reasons for the consulting boom
- the kinds of people who should consider the consulting option
- establishing yourself as an expert
- exploiting the media to promote yourself and your business
- getting a first assignment
- building a Supergroup of Independent Contractors
- expanding into related fields
- negotiating for success
- how and where to set up your office
- the legal form for your consulting business

LANT IN DENVER, Page 2

Since January when THE CONSULTANT'S KIT was first published, Lant
has been interviewed by at least one media outlet every day. He has
been interviewed by NBC radio, CBS radio, the National Black Radio
Network, the Associated Press, Joe Franklin Show (WOR-TV, New York),
and major media in: Boston, Los Angeles, Pittsburgh, Detroit, and
Connecticut. Each time the listener response has been extraordinary.
In part this is because of Lant himself. "Lant's own style is fascina-
ting," writes the Hartford Advocate; in part, it's because of the
importance of the subject which, Lant feels, is indicative of a permanent change in the way Americans are working and living.

The 35-year-old Harvard-educated Lant is president of a Cambridge,
Massachusetts consulting firm for nonprofit organizations. He is also
the Editor of a newly-published (June) volume entitled OUR HARVARD:
REFLECTIONS ON COLLEGE LIFE BY TWENTY-TWO DISTINGUISHED GRADUATES
(Taplinger). It includes the original contributions of Buckminster
Fuller, Erich Segal, Arthur Schlesinger, Robert Coles and other
eminent Harvard men. Lant is also the author of DEVELOPMENT TODAY: A
GUIDE FOR NONPROFIT ORGANIZATIONS and INSUBSTANTIAL PAGEANT: CEREMONY
AND CONFUSION AT QUEEN VICTORIA'S COURT. His in-progress book is
entitled THE UNABASHED SELF-PROMOTER'S GUIDE and will be published
in Winter, 1983.

Lant is included in Who's Who in the East, Men & Women of Distinction, The Dictionary of International Biography, The Book of Honor,
and The International Who's Who of Intellectuals.

To arrange a convenient interview time, please call Mel Anderson
at (303) 973-5127 or Jeffrey Lant directly at (617) 547-6372. Photographs and review copies of THE CONSULTANT'S KIT are available upon
request.

Available interview dates in Denver for Dr Jeffrey Lant:

- Sunday evening, October 3   - Friday evening, November 5
- Monday evening, October 4
- all day Tuesday, October 5

Essentials of an Announcement to an Alumni, Business, or Trade-Association Publication

- Place the announcement on a sheet of your stationery or in a letter to the editor of the publication.
- Peruse the publication to ensure that you use the correct format.
- Immediately mention your connection with the organization, stating, for example, that you are a graduate of the Class of 1956.
- Include an address to which people can respond.
- Place announcements every six months, if possible.

Sample Announcement

Mr. John Williams, Editor
Tufts Observer
287 Wayland Ave.
Medford, MA 02128

Dear Mr. Williams:

As a graduate of Tufts' Class of 1976, I would be grateful if you'd run the following paragraph in the *Observer* to alert classmates and friends to my new business.

> Peter Grady, Class of 1976, announces the formation of his new management consulting firm, Grady Associates, Inc. Peter will focus on providing technical assistance to small businesses. He can be reached at 401 Dwight Avenue, Swampscott, Mass. 01897 for further information.

Thank you for your consideration.

Sincerely,

Peter Grady

Essentials of a Proposal

- Present the proposal in a memorandum or a letter.
- If you use a memo, use the block format.
- Begin with the title of the project.
- Include a brief project description in the first paragraph.
- Detail the project's purpose.
- Suggest from the client's viewpoint why the project is needed.
- Suggest why the company or organization to whom you propose the project is best for it.
- Suggest a first step in realizing the project.
- How long will the project take? Determine the project's length, focusing on the completion of a first stage.
- State your relationship to the project.
- Suggest a follow up to this communication.

Sample Proposal

To: Peter D. Smith, Dean, Professional Management Institute, Inc.
From: John K. Malone, President, Nonprofit Associates, Inc.
Re: Development of a Nonprofit Organization Management Program
Date: June 15, 1981

Title: Nonprofit Organization Management Program

Brief project description: Development of a certificate program in nonprofit-organization management.

Purpose: To prepare executive directors, chairmen of the board, trustees, and employees of nonprofit organizations in significant areas of nonprofit management.

Why this program is needed: Individuals often become executives and trustees of nonprofit organizations without having adequate management training. They may be specialists in the technical work of their agency, but not in the business of keeping an organization sound. Such personnel are often trained on the job to the detriment of their agencies. On-the-job training is particularly costly, and the demands of running an agency are great.

The proposal: To establish an intensive training program for nonprofit executives and aspiring executives.

Suggested Curriculum: The intensive program might include courses in: organizational behavior, management, personnel policy, fund raising and development, bookkeeping and accounting, law and the nonprofit organization, program development and review, and the role of the board of trustees.

Why the Professional Management Institute: The Professional Management Institute already offers basic courses to professionals in a wide variety of fields. This proposal simply extends the work of the Institute into a compatible area.

Suggested first step: To form a broad-based committee to consider the advisability of establishing such a program. This committee might be composed of administrators from the Institute, two or three executive directors of local nonprofit organizations, one or two possible instructors in the program, and the representative of a local foundation, which might ultimately be induced to fund the program. This committee, working with consultants, might produce a suitable proposal for presentations to foundations and corporations with a request for pilot, start-up funds.

Time frame: This committee should be appointed during the month of June. Meetings should be held throughout the summer. The proposal should be ready for submission to potential funding sources in September. The first intensive session could begin in January, 1982.

Relationship of Nonprofit Associates, Inc. to the Project: The project was first proposed by Nonprofit Associates, Inc. to you during a general session in which we discussed the possibility of being retained by the Institute. We now propose to work with you in conceiving and actualizing the Nonprofit Organization Management Program.

Follow-Up to this Memorandum: I shall call you in 10 days to discuss this matter.

Essentials of the Client Letter of Intent

- Address the letter to the person who will sign the document.
- If you send this letter to follow up a meeting or telephone conversation at which details of the deal were settled, mention the date of the meeting.
- Detail your duties and responsibilities in the second paragraph. Define your duties and responsibilities broadly.
- Also include the date by which your work is to be completed in the second paragraph.
- Detail the responsibilities of the client to you in the third paragraph, stating, for example, that he will provide you with office space and secretarial assistance.
- Mention financial consideration in the fourth paragraph, including how much you will be paid, in what way, and how your expenses will be handled.
- Allow space at the foot of the document for the client's signature.

Mr. Charles Peabody, Executive Director
Cambridge Preservation Alliance, Inc.
136 Bigelow Street
Cambridge, MA 02139

Dear Mr. Peabody:

This letter follows our telephone conversation of June 3, 1981, in which we discussed my consulting relationship with the Cambridge Preservation Alliance.

It is my understanding that in that conversation we agreed I should be retained by the Alliance for the period between June 15, 1981, and September 15, 1981. My duties include the preparation of the Annual Report of the Alliance, drafting a new membership brochure, and the preparation of no fewer than two or more than four development proposals suitable for submission to private foundations and corporations.

I understand that I shall provide all copy for these documents, and that the final copy will be typed by a secretary provided by the Alliance.

For my work, the Alliance will pay me $1000; $250.00 of this amount is due upon signature, and $250 is due each month for next three months, on or before the 15th day of the month. In addition, the Alliance will pay me for all customary and reasonable expenses, including travel, copying ,and postage. Any such expenditure more than $10, however, must be approved by you.

If your understanding parallels mine, please sign one copy of this document and return it to me along with your check for $250.

I look forward to working with you on this important project.

Sincerely,

Consultant

Accepted:

CAMBRIDGE PRESERVATION ALLIANCE
By: _____
    Charles Peabody, Executive Director
Date of Acceptance: _____

Essentials of a Letter of Intent to a Sub-Contractor

- If you send this letter to follow up a meeting or telephone call at which details of the deal were decided, mention the date of conversation.

- Outline the duties and responsibilities of the sub-contractor in the second paragraph. Specifically spell out what you expect of the sub-contractor and when.

- Allow sufficient time to review the work of the sub-contractor before giving it to your client because it may be necessary to revise some of the work.

- List in paragraph three your responsiblities to the sub-contractor beyond the matter of consideration.

- Detail in the fourth paragraph all matters of financial consideration: how much you will pay, in what way, and how expenses will be handled.

- Mention in paragraph five the relationship of the sub-contractor to the client, stating, for example, that what the sub-contractor learns while working on this project is confidential.

- If the sub-contractor has not signed a noncompetitive agreement with you, have him do so or enclose a paragraph about it in this letter.

- Allow space at the foot of the letter for the sub-contractor's signature.

Sample Sub-Contractor Letter of Intent

Ms. Jane Miles
136 Appian Way
Cambridge, Mass. 02138

Dear Jane,

This letter follows our telephone conversation of June 4, 1981, in which we discussed my project with the Cambridge Preservation Alliance.

In that conversation, we agreed that you would prepare several documents relating to the work of the Alliance, namely an annual report, a new membership brochure, and no fewer than two nor more than four development proposals for submission to private foundations and corporations.

You have agreed to present me with camera-ready copy, typed double-spaced for these documents on or before the following dates, with copy to be of the following lengths:
    Annual Report: July 1, 1981, 5,000 words
    Membership Brochure: August 1, 1981 approximately
      2,000 words
    Between two and four development proposals: the first
      to be finished on or before August 15, 1981, the others due thereafter on dates to
      be arranged, all with lengths of 2,000 to 3,000 words.

For this work, I will pay you $600 (six hundred dollars), $200 upon satisfactory completion of the annual report, $200 upon completion of the membership brochure, and the final $200 upon completion of the last development proposal. You can bill me for copying, travel, and postage expenses; receipts are due on or about the last Friday of any month for payment within 30 days.

All materials and information gathered by you in connection with this project are confidential, and in signing this letter, you agree that no use shall be made of the information beyond the terms of your engagement.

Please sign one copy of this letter and return it to me.

I look forward to working with you on this project.

Sincerely,

Consultant

Accepted: _____   Date: _____
      Jane Miles

Essentials of a Contract

(Note: I have selected as a sample a standard JLA "Professional Fund-Raising Counsel Contract." Contracts vary widely. This sample however, provides you with a model that you can adapt for your own contract.)

Section I: Introduction

- Title
- Date of agreement
- List of parties
- Brief description of applicable work of consultant
- Indication that client wishes to purchase this particular aspect of the consultant's work

Section II: Services provided by consultant

- List of services

Section III: Special responsibilities of client to consultant

- List of special responsibilities

Section IV: Fees

- How much will consultant be paid
- The payment schedule
- Penalty for sums in arrears
- Client default clause
- Litigation clause

Section V: General conditions

- Consultant's best-effort clause
- Client allows consultant reasonable access to material and personnel
- No-guarantee clause
- Expenses clause. What will client pay for?
  When? What happens if the amount owed is in arrears?

Section VI: Conclusion

- How long will contract be in effect?
- What is the applicable law?
- Signatures

Sample Contract

Professional Fund-Raising Counsel Contract with Jeffrey Lant Associates, Inc .

This Agreement, entered into this   day of   , 1981, by and between Jeffrey Lant Associates, Inc. (hereinafter referred to a JLA) and   (hereinafter referred to as Client) WITNESSETH AS FOLLOWS:

Whereas JLA is organized to assist nonprofit organizations in fund-raising activities; whereas client is a nonprofit organization interested in purchasing the services of JLA, NOW, THEREFORE, it is agreed between the parties as follows:

I. Services Provided by JLA

a) Review Client's past corporate, foundation, and individual fund-raising efforts, including past proposals, solicitation letters, and supplementary materials;

b) Examine Client's programs to determine fundability and marketability;

c) Meet with adminstration and staff to establish development priorities;

d) Conduct a workshop with board members, staff, and volunteers to elicit information on possible funding source leads;

e) Provide an individual memorandum for each participant explaining how to use such information, once gathered;

f) Draft necessary development document(s) for private funding sources;

g) Repeat any and all aspects of the above process on an as-needed basis for duration of contract;

h) Identify corporations, foundations, and individuals who may be potential donors;

i) Draft solicitation letters to personal contributors and advise on their use;

j) Draft invitation letters to social and information sessions to which corporation, foundation, and potential individual donors will be invited;

k) Advise on the organization of all aspects of these situations, including organizational presentations to be made and role of Client staff;

l) Work with organizational representatives to define best approaches to all prospective donors;

n) Meet regularly with organizational representatives, generally for one to two hours a week, to advise on all development business, including reviewing pending development proposals, handling correspondence, and advising on meetings with potential funding sources;

n) Supply a copy of *Development Today: A Guide for Nonprofit Organizations* by Dr. Jeffrey Lant;

o) Maintain an "on-call" position with Client for duration of contract.

Section II: Fees

Client agrees to pay JLA _____. Payment shall be made in the following way: _____
_____ If any payment as per the above schedule is more than 30 days in arrears, Client hereby authorizes JLA to charge Client a one and one-half percent (1½%) per month penalty on the amount in arrears.

If any payment as per the above schedule is more than 60 days in arrears, Client hereby additionally authorizes JLA to declare Client to be in default under this agreement. In such event, JLA may, in its sole discretion, declare the entire unpaid total of payments owed under this agreement immediately due and payable and shall suspend services to the Client until such time as the outstanding balance is rendered.

If the outstanding balance remains overdue for more than 60 days, Client acknowledges that JLA may take legal action to collect the overdue amount. In such event, Client will be responsible for all reasonable litigation expenses incurred by JLA, including but not limited to court costs and attorney fees.

Section III: General Conditions

a) JLA agrees to use its best efforts to perform the services listed in Paragraph #1 above;

b) Client agrees to allow JLA reasonable access to Client's place of business, staff members, books, and records to permit JLA to perform its services as fully and economically as possible. Client further agrees to cooperate with JLA on all reasonable requests made by JLA for the mutual benefits of the parties hereto;

c) Client understands and acknowledges that JLA has made no guarantee of funding and that JLA has made no express or implied warranties apart from this agreement;

d) Client shall be responsible for all reasonable disbursements of JLA on behalf of Client, including travel and accommodations, long-distance telephone calls, copy costs, and postage. JLA agrees to seek Client's prior approval on any major disbursements of more that $10. JLA agrees to bill Client for disbursements on a regular basis, and Client agrees to pay said bills within 30 days of their receipt. Said bills not so paid after 30 days will be subject to a one and one-half-percent (1½%) per-month penalty on the amount in arrears.

Section IV: Conclusion

This agreement, executed in duplicate, shall remain in effect for _____ from the date of signing. It sets forth the entire contract between the parties and may be cancelled, modified, or amended only by a written instrument executed by each of the parties thereto.

This agreement shall be construed as a Massachusetts contract.

WITNESS the hands and seals of the parties hereto, each duly authorized, the day and year first written above.

JEFFREY LANT ASSOCIATES, INC.

By: _____
     Jeffrey L. Lant, President
CLIENT NAME
By: _____

Additional Essentials of a Commission Contract

Note: From a consultant's standpoint a commission contract varies in two important respects from a fixed, flat fee contract. Sections must be added that:

- Detail the responsibilities of the client to the consultant, and
- Guarantee the right of the consultant to have access to available information that will allow him to determine if he has been paid all allowable commissions from his work.

If the preceding professional fund-raising counsel contract involved payment by commission instead of a fixed, flat fee, the following essential points would appear in the contract:

Section III: Responsibilities of client

- Acknowledgement of client responsibilities
- List of specific responsibilities

Section IV: Fees

- Commission the consultant will receive
- In-kind appraisal process
- When commission payments are due
- Interest on overdue amounts owed consultant

Section V: General conditions

- Consultant is allowed access to client books.
- Consultant owns materials generated during his relationship with client.
- Client acknowledges responsibility to share with consultant pertinent correspondence and other materials that relate to determining the consultant's success and the payment of applicable commissions.

Additional Language for a Commission Contract

Section III: Responsibilities of Client

    a) Client acknowledges that this arrangement with JLA is a collaborative one and therefore undertakes to work diligently with JLA to realize its goals.

    b) Client agrees to use its best efforts to use its board of directors, staff, volunteers, and friends in the development process outlined by JLA;

    c) Client agrees to hold regularly scheduled workshop sessions at the direction of JLA;

    d) Client agrees to urge those participating in these workshops to complete assigned tasks for the mutual benefit of the parties hereto;

    e) Client agrees to hold regular sessions with the representatives of corporations, foundations, and potential individual donors at the direction of JLA.

Section IV: Fees

- Client agrees to pay JLA for any funds or in-kind donations received by Client as the direct result of JLA's services.

- In each calendar year, this payment shall be (percentage) of all such funds received or in-kind donations.

- In the case of an in-kind donation, the value thereof shall be determined by an appraisal process to be agreed upon by JLA and the client at the time;

- Payment of the fee shall be made by the Client to JLA within 10 business days after any such funds are received by client or after the in-kind donation appraisal has taken place.

- If such fees are not paid to JLA within the specified time, Client acknowledges JLA's right to charge Client interest at the rate of one and one-half percent (1½%) for each month said payment is overdue.

Section V: General Conditions

- Client allows JLA reasonable access to Client's place of business, staff, books, and records in order to assist JLA in its performance under this contract. Client further agrees to permit JLA or its agent to inspect relevant books and materials at the end of JLA's engagement with Client or at any time during said engagement.

- All materials, memoranda, letters, communications, proposals, and applications generated by JLA shall be and remain its exclusive property and any use of the same by Client without the express permission of JLA is hereby prohibited.

- Client agrees to provide or make available to JLA copies of all correspondence from any foundation, corporation, or individual funding source contacted by Client as a direct result of JLA's performance.

Essentials of an Independent Contractor Contract

Section I: Parties and their relationship

- A list of parties and a description of relevant aspect of business
- Disclaimer of any agent or employee relationship

Section II: Duties of the independent contractor

- What the independent contractor will do
- Date assignment is to be completed

Section III: Consideration

- How much will contracting party pay independent contractor
- Applicable expenses

Section IV: Cancellation

- How can this contract be cancelled?

Section V: Confidentiality

- Materials gathered from the contracting party's client are to be returned by the independent contractor and are to be treated as confidential.

Section VI: Noncompetitive clause

- Limitations placed on approach of independent contractor to contracting party's clients

Section VII: Assignability

- How may the contracting parties assign their rights?

Section IX: Term of Contract

- When will contract begin and how long does it remain in effect?

Section X: Integration

- Contract to be executed in duplicate
- How contract may be cancelled, modified, or amended
- Date of signing
- Signatures of parties

Sample Contract for Performance of Independent Contractor Services

This is a contract between ABC Corporation, Inc., of 11 Waterhouse Avenue, Burlington, Iowa, 40505, herein referred to as ABC, and _____ (contractor's name) and (address), _____ herein referred to as "contractor," for the performance of the services described below.

Section I: Parties and relationship

ABC is an Iowa corporation engaged in part in the business of supplying technical assistance to small businesses through the use of skilled independent contractors; (contractor's name) is a person who by education, training or experience is skilled in providing (service). The parties intend that an independent contractor-employer relationship be created by this contract. Contractor is not to be considered an agent or employee of ABC for any purpose.

Section II: Duties

ABC agrees to provide contractor with the following assignment:
(List of contractor responsibilities)
In accepting the above assignment, contractor agrees to use diligence and professional skill in the completion of all tasks. Contractor further agrees to submit the work in question, in finished, professional quality form, to ABC on or before (date).

Section III: Consideration

Upon timely receipt of the aforementioned material, ABC agrees to pay contractor the sum of (amount). The parties agree that no payment shall be made for contractor's meals, travel costs, travel time, accommodations, telephone calls, stationery, supplies, etc.

Section IV: Cancellation

The parties agree that this contract is not subject to cancellation, except in the event that (contracting party's client) withdraws its request for the project described above. In such event this contract will be cancelled as of the date the contractor can be reasonably notified of such withdrawal. ABC agrees to pay contractor for all days and fractions of days actually worked, at the rate described above, prior to such notification.

Section V: Confidentiality

It is understood that in the performance of his duties, contractor will obtain information about both ABC and (contracting party's client), and that such information may include financial data, client lists, methods of operation, policy statement, and other confidential data.

Contractor agrees to restrict his use of such information to the performance of duties described in this contract. Contractor further agrees to return to ABC and to (contracting party's client) upon the completion of his duties any and all documents (originals and copies) taken from either organization to facilitate the project described above.

Section VI: Noncompetitive Clause

Contractor further agrees that he will not perform his professional services for any organization known to contractor to be a client of ABC unless ABC has employed contractor for the provision of such services to the client. This restriction shall remain in effect for a period of two years after the termination of this contract. For the purposes of this section, "client" is defined as any organization, which during said period of restriction, has engaged ABC to provide:
(list of all services provided by contracting party)

Section VII: Applicable law

The parties agree that this contract is to be construed as an Iowa contract.

Section VIII: Assignability

Neither party can assign or delegate its rights or duties under this contract without the express, written consent of the other party.

Section IX: Term of contract

This contract will become effective immediately and shall remain in effect until the promises and duties described herein have been fully performed.

Section X: Integration

This contract, executed in duplicate, sets forth the entire contract between the parties and may be cancelled, modified, or amended only by a written instrument executed by each of the parties here, or as specifically provided in this contract.

WITNESS the hands and seals of the parties hereto, each duly authorized, this _____ day of 1981.

ABC Corporation

By _____
    James W. Turner, President

_____
    Independent Contractor Name

Essentials of a Workshop Contract

(This is a standard contract between a consultant and a co-sponsoring organization.)

Section I: Parties: List the parties involved

Section II: Relationship of parties

Section III: Duties of parties

- When will client produce the workshop?
- How will the client promote the workshop?
- What will the client provide for the workshop in terms of space, refreshments, and personnel?
- What materials will the consultant supply to registrants?
- What sample brochures will the consultant supply for promotional purposes?
- Who will conduct the workshop?

Section IV: Registration, attendance, fees

- Who will participate?
- How many participants will there be?
- What will participants pay?

Section V: Consideration, deductible expenses

- The consultant's fee
- List of expenses

Section VI: Withdrawal, cancellation, notices, damages

- Notice of intent to withdraw
- When liquidated damages do not apply
- When liquidated damages apply
- In case of severely bad weather
- Who bears the cost if workshop is cancelled

Section VII: Assignability
- How parties to this contract can delegate their rights

Section VIII:

- Applicable law: Which state law is applicable?

Section IX: Integration

- Contract to be executed in duplicate
- How to cancel, modify, or amend the contract
- Date of signature
- Signatures of parties

Development Training Workshop Contract

Jeffrey Lant Associates Inc. ("JLA") and _____
("_____"), for consideration detailed herein, agree to
produce, present, and co-sponsor a Development Training Workshop ("Workshop") under the
terms and conditions of this contract.

Section I: Parties

JLA is a Massachusetts corporation with its principal place of business at 50 Follen Street,
Suite 507, Cambridge, Massachusetts 02138.

_____ is a _____ located at

_____

Section II: Relationship of Parties

_____ does hereby employ JLA as an independent contractor that
will provide professional services and products to _____ , as specified
herein. The parties agree that JLA will have the right to provide similar services and products to
other employers at any time, except when actually providing them to
_____ on the date specified herein.

Section III: Duties of parties

1. _____ agrees to co-sponsor a Workshop, which will be held on the
_____ day of _____ , 19____, between the hours of _____ and _____, at
_____ .

2. Prior to the date of the Workshop, _____ agrees to use all reasonable
means to promote and publicize the Workshop, including, but not limited to, direct mailings of
informational materials to potential registrants, advertisements or listings in professional
publications, and notices directed to the general public.

3. On the date of the Workshop, _____ agrees to provide:
   a. A room, hall, auditorium, or similar space, which, if sufficiently large, will be
      equipped with a microphone;
   b. Lunch to all registrants;

c. Qualified personnel to process registration, introduce the Workshop Leader, and serve lunch.

4. On or before the date of the Workshop, JLA agrees to provide to _____ *Development Today: A Guide for Nonprofit Organizations,* by Dr. Jeffrey L. Lant, in a quantity sufficient to supply each registrant with a copy.

5. JLA agrees to provide, on the date of the Workshop, Dr. Jeffrey L. Lant, who will serve as the Workshop Leader, in which capacity he will teach and advise the registrants, answer their questions, promote discussion, and perform other appropriate and customary functions.

Section IV: Registration, attendance, fees

The parties agree that the Workshop will be open only to those who have officially registered, either in advance or on the day of the Workshop, and who have paid the entire registration fee, except that _____ may permit as many as three of its officers, directors, staff, or students (when applicable) to attend the Workshop free of charge.

The parties agree that the number of registrants will be limited to _____.

The parties agree that the registration fee for the Workshop will be $_____ if lunch is served and $_____ if lunch is not served.

Section V: Consideration, deductible expenses

The parties agree that JLA and _____ shall divide evenly the net proceeds of the Workshop, except that in no event shall JLA receive less than _____ , so long as the Workshop is actually held.

In this agreement, "net proceeds" is defined as total proceeds (from registation fees) minus deductible expenses.

Deductible expenses are limited to the following:

a) _____'s actual expenses in providing lunch to all registrants, but not to exceed $5 per registrant;

b) Necessary, proper, and customary travel and accommodation expenses for Dr. Jeffrey Lant, including air and ground transportation, meals, and hotel or motel charges;

c) Expense of printing Workshop brochure;

d) Expense of mailing Workshop brochure to potential registrants;

e) Expense of the JLA Development workbook, the cost to be figured as _____ per workbook supplied, except that JLA will supply this workbook without cost to the aforementioned enrolled officers, directors, staff, and students (when applicable) of the co-sponsor.

Section VI: Withdrawal, cancellation, notice, damages

The parties agree that the withdrawal of either party from the workshop shall be subject to the following conditions:

a) Notice of intent to withdraw must be communicated in a timely manner to the other party. Communication may be by telephone, telegraph, or registered mail;

b) If said communication is received by the other party 30 or more days before the scheduled date of the Workshop, this entire contract shall be cancelled and the party withdrawing shall be assessed no damages;

c) If said communication is received fewer than 30 days before the scheduled date of the Workshop, this entire contract will be cancelled, but the party withdrawing shall pay liquidated damages of $250 to the other party, except that in the case of severely bad weather conditions or natural disaster, _____ , with the consent of JLA, may postpone the Workshop to a time mutually agreeable to the parties, without the assessment damages;

d) In the event that the Workshop is for any reason postponed or cancelled, _____ agrees to bear any and all costs of refunding deposits or fees to registrants.

Section VII: Assignability

Neither party may assign or delegate its rights under this contract without the express, written consent of the other party.

Section VIII: Applicable Law

The parties agree that this contract is to be construed as a Massachusetts contract.

Section IX: Integration

This contract, executed in duplicate, sets forth the entire contract between the parties and may be cancelled, modified, or amended only by a written instrument executed by each of the parties hereto, or as specifically provided in this contract.

WITNESS the hands and seals of the parties hereto, each duly authorized, this _____ day of _____, 19_____.

Jeffrey Lant Associates, Inc.

By: _____
   Jeffrey L. Lant, President

Client Name _____

By: _____

Office: _____

Essentials of the Corporate By-Laws

(Note: For purposes of illustration, I have used a standard set of Massachusetts corporate by-laws. Corporate laws vary in each state, although major provisions are standard. To ascertain the by-laws needed by your corporation, check with your lawyer.)

Section I: Articles of organization: The powers of the corporation, its officers and directors are set forth in the articles of organization.

Section II: Rights and powers of the corporate stockholders

- Annual meeting: When will it be held?
- Special meeting in place of the annual meeting: how to hold it.
- Other special meetings: how to call them.
- Place of meetings: where should they be held?
- Notice of meetings: How much notification time?
- Quorum of stockholders: What constitutes a quorum?
- Action by vote: when stockholders are present, how many are needed to vote?
- Voting: who is eligible to vote?
- Action by writing: when stockholders are not present, how to pass matters by written communication.
- Proxies: stockholders may present valid substitutes for themselves.

Section III: Powers and duties of the board of directors

- Members: how many directors will there be?
- Tenure: how long do they serve?
- Powers: what can they do?
- Committees: what Committees will there be, how will they be composed?
- Regular meetings: how to call them.
- Special meetings: how to call them.
- Notice: how much notification time is required?
- Quorum: how many Directors must be present to transact business?
- Action by vote: how many directors must be present to take action?
- Action by writing: how can the directors take action through written communications?

Section IV: Officers and agents of the corporation

- Enumeration and qualification: how many officers will there be and what must their qualifications be?
- Powers: what can they do?
- Election: how will the officers be elected?
- Tenure: how long do they serve?
- President and vice president: their powers and duties
- Clerk and assistant clerks: their powers and duties

Section V: Resignations and removals

- How the resignation and removal of officers and directors is to be handled.

Section VI: Vacancies

- How vacancies of officers and directors are to be handled.

Section VII: Capital stock

- Stock certificates: particulars relating to stock certificates.
- Loss of Certificates: issuing of duplicate certificates.

Section VIII: Transfer of shares of stock

- Transfer on books: relating to the stockholders of record.
- Record date and closing transfer books: The date that determines stockholder eligibility for matters such as dividends and distributions to stockholders.

Section IX: Indemnification of Directors and Officers

- Corporation can vote stipends to directors and officers.

Section X: Corporate seal

- Particulars of the corporate seal.

Section XI: Execution of papers

- Who shall be able to execute legal papers of the corporation.

Section XII: Amendments

- Outlines how the articles of organization can be amended.

BY-LAWS
of
XYZ Corporation

Section 1. Articles of organization

These by-laws, the powers of the corporation and of its directors and stockholders, and all matters concerning the regulation of the corporation's business shall be subject to such provisions as are set forth in the Articles of Organization.

Section 2. Stockholders

2.1. *Annual Meeting.* The annual meeting of the stockholders shall be held at 10:00 o'clock in the forenoon on the third Thursday in August in each year, unless a different hour is fixed by the president or the directors. If that day be a legal holiday at the place in which the meeting is to be held, the meeting shall be held on the next succeeding day not a legal holiday at such place. Purposes for which an annual meeting is to be held, additional to those prescribed by law, by the Articles of Organization or by these by-laws, may be specified by the president or by the directors.

2.2. *Special Meeting in Place of Annual Meeting.* If no annual meeting has been held in accordance with the foregoing provisions, a special meeting of the stockholders can be held in place thereof, and any action taken at such special meeting shall have the same force and effect as if taken at the annual meeting, and in such case all references in these by-laws to the annual meeting of the stockholders shall be deemed to refer to such special meeting. Any such special meeting shall be called as provided in Section 2.3.

2.3 *Special Meetings.* A special meeting of the stockholders may be called at any time by the president or by the directors. Each call of a meeting shall state the place, date, hour and purposes of the meeting.

2.4. *Place of Meetings.* All meetings of the stockholders shall be held at the principal office of the corporation in Massachusetts or at such other place within the United States as shall be fixed by the president or the directors. Any adjourned session of any meeting of the stockholders shall be held at the same city or town as the initial session, or within Massachusetts, in either case at the place designated in the vote of adjournment.

2.5 *Notice of Meetings.* A written notice of each meeting of stockholders, stating the place, date, and hour and the purposes of the meeting, shall be given at least seven days before the meeting to each stockholder entitled to vote thereat and to each stockholder who, by law, by the articles of organization or by these by-laws, is entitled to notice, by leaving such notice with him or at his residence or usual place of business, or by mailing it to such stockholder at his address as it appears in the records of the corporation. Such notice shall be given by the clerk or an assistant clerk or by an officer designated by the directors. No notice of any meeting of stockholders need be given to a stockholder if a written waiver of notice, executed before or after the meeting by such stockholder or his attorney thereunto duly authorized, is filed with the records of the meeting.

2.6 *Quorum of Stockholders.* At any meeting of the stockholders, a quorum shall consist of a majority in interest of all stock issued and outstanding and entitled to vote at the meeting. Stock owned directly or indirectly by the corporation, if any, shall not be deemed outstanding for this purpose. Any meeting may be adjourned from time to time by a majority of the votes properly cast upon the question, whether or not a quorum is present, and the meeting may be held as adjourned without further notice.

2.7. *Action by Vote.* When a quorum is present at any meeting, a plurality of the votes properly cast for election to any office shall elect to such office, and a majority of the votes properly cast upon any question, except when a larger vote is required by law. No ballot shall be required for any election unless requested by a stockholder present or represented at the meeting and entitled to vote in the election.

2.8. *Voting.* Stockholders entitled to vote shall have one vote for each share of stock entitled to vote held by them of record according to the records of the corporation, unless otherwise provided by the articles of organization. The corporation shall not, directly or indirectly, vote any share of its own.

2.9. *Action by Writing.* Any action to be taken by stockholders may be taken without a meeting if all stockholders entitled to vote on the matter consent to the action by a writing filed with the records of the meetings of stockholders. Such consent shall be treated for all purposes as a vote at a meeting.

2.10. *Proxies.* Stockholders entitled to vote may vote either in person or by proxy in writing dated not more than two months before the meeting named therein, which proxies shall be filed with the clerk or other person responsible to record the proceedings of the meeting before being voted. Unless otherwise specifically limited by their terms, such proxies shall entitle the holders thereof to vote at any adjournment of such meeting but shall not be valid after the final adjournment of such meeting.

Section 3. Board of Directors

3.1. *Number.* A board of not more than seven nor fewer than one directors shall be elected at the annual meeting of the stockholders, by such stockholders as have the right to vote at such election. The number of directors may be increased at any time or from time to time either by the stockholders or by the directors by vote of a majority of the directors then in office. The number of directors may be decreased to any number not fewer than one at any time or from time to time either by the stockholders or by the directors by a vote of a majority of the directors then in office, but only to eliminate vacancies existing by reason of death, resignation or removal of one or more directors. No director need be a stockholder.

3.2 *Tenure.* Except as otherwise provided by law, by the articles of organization or by these by-laws, the directors shall hold office until the next annual meeting of the stockholders and until their successors are elected and qualified, or until a director sooner dies, resigns, is removed or becomes disqualified.

3.3 *Powers.* Except as reserved to the stockholders by law, by the articles of organization or by these by-laws, the business of the corporation shall be managed by the directors who shall have all the powers of the corporation. In particular, and without limiting the generality of the foregoing, the directors may at any time issue all or from time to time any part of the unissued capital stock of the corporation from time to time authorized under the articles of organization and may determine, subject to any requirements of law, the consideration for which stock is to be issued and the manner of allocating such consideration between capital and surplus.

3.4 *Committees.* The directors may, by vote of a majority of the directors then in office, elect from their number an executive committee and other committees and may by vote delegate to any such committee or committees some or all of the powers of the directors except those which by law, by the articles of organization or by these by-laws they are prohibited from delegating. Except as the directors may otherwise determine, any such committee may make rules for the conduct of its business, but unless otherwise provided by the directors or such rules, its business shall be conducted as nearly as may be in the same manner as is provided by these by-laws for the conduct of business by the directors.

3.5. *Regular Meetings*. Regular meetings of the directors may be held without call or notice at such places and at such times as the directors may from time to time determine, provided that notice of the first regular meeting following any such determination shall be given to absent directors. A regular meeting of the directors may be held without call or notice immediately after and at the same place as the annual meeting of the stockholders.

3.6. *Special Meetings*. Special meetings of the directors may be held at any time and at any place designated in the call of the meeting, when called by the president or the treasurer, reasonable notice thereof being given to each director by the secretary or an assistant secretary, or, if there be none, by the clerk or an assistant clerk, or by the officer calling the meeting.

3.7. *Notice*. It shall be sufficient notice to a director to send notice by mail at least 48 hours or by telegram at least 24 hours before the meeting. Notice of a meeting need not be given to any director if a written waiver of notice, executed by him before or after the meeting, is filed with the records of the meeting, or to any director who attends the meeting without protesting prior thereto or at its commencement the lack of notice to him. Neither notice of a meeting nor a waiver of a notice need specify the purposes of the meeting.

3.8. *Quorum*. At any meeting of the directors a majority of the directors then in office shall constitute a quorum. Any meeting may be adjourned from time to time by a majority of the votes cast upon the question, whether or not a quorum is present, and the meeting may be held as adjourned without further notice.

3.9. *Action by Vote*. When a quorum is present at any meeting, a majority of the directors present may take any action, except when a larger vote is required by law.

3.10. *Action by Writing*. Any action required or permitted to be taken at any meeting of the directors may be taken without a meeting if a written consent thereto is signed by all the directors and such written consent is filed with the records of the meetings of the directors. Such consent shall be treated for all purposes as a vote at a meeting.

Section 4. Officers and Agents

4.1 *Enumeration, Qualification.* The officers of the corporation shall be a president, a treasurer, a clerk, and such other officers, if any, as the incorporators at their initial meeting, or the directors from time to time, may in their discretion elect or appoint. The corporation may also have such agents, if any, as the incorporators at their initial meeting, or the directors from time to time, may in their discretion appoint. Any officer may be, but none needs be, a director or stockholder. The clerk shall be a resident of Massachusetts unless the corporation has a resident agent appointed for the purpose of service of process. Any two or more offices may be held by the same person. Any officer may be required by the directors to give bond for the faithful performance of his duties to the corporation in such amount and with such sureties as the directors may determine.

4.2. *Powers.* Subject to law, to the articles of organization and to the other provisions of these by-laws, each officer shall have, in addition to the duties and powers herein set forth, such duties and powers as are commonly incident to his office and such duties and powers as the directors may from time to time designate.

4.3. *Election.* The president, the treasurer, and the clerk shall be elected annually by the directors at their first meeting following the annual meeting of the stockholders. Other officers, if any, may be elected or appointed by the board of directors at said meeting or at any other time.

4.4. *Tenure.* Except as otherwise provided by law or by the articles of organization or by these by-laws, the president, the treasurer, and the clerk shall hold office until the first meeting of the directors following the next annual meeting of the stockholders and until their respective successors are chosen and qualified, and each other officer shall hold office until the first meeting of the stockholders unless a shorter period shall have been specified by the terms of his election or appointment, or in each case until he sooner dies, resigns, is removed or becomes disqualified. Each agent shall retain his authority at the pleasure of the directors.

4.5. *President and Vice Presidents.* The president shall be the chief executive officer of the corporation and, subject to the control of the directors, shall have general charge and supervision of the business of the corporation. The president shall preside at all meetings of the stockholders and of the directors at which he is present, except as otherwise voted by the directors. Any vice presidents shall have such duties and powers as shall be designated from time to time by the directors.

4.6. *Treasurer and Assistant Treasurers.* The treasurer shall be the chief financial and accounting officer of the corporation and shall be in charge of its funds and valuable papers, books of account and accounting records, and shall have such other duties and powers as may be designated from time to time by the directors or by the president.

Any assistant treasurers shall have such duties and powers as shall be designated from time to time by the directors.

4.7. *Clerk and Assistant Clerks.* The clerk shall record all proceedings of the stockholders in a book or series of books to be kept therefore, which book or books shall be kept at the principal office of the corporation or at the office of its transfer agent or of its clerk and shall be open at all reasonable times to the inspection of any stockholder. In the absence of the clerk from any meeting of stockholder, an assistant clerk, or if there be none or he is absent, a temporary clerk chosen at the meeting, shall record the proceedings thereof in the aforesaid book. Unless a transfer agent has been appointed the clerk shall keep or cause to be kept the stock and transfer records of the corporation, which shall contain the names and record addresses of all stockholders and the amount of stock held by each. If no secretary is elected, the clerk shall keep a true record of the proceedings of all meetings of the directors and in his absence from any such meeting an assistant clerk, or if there be none or he is absent, a temporary clerk chosen at the meeting, shall record the proceedings thereof.

Any assistant clerk shall have such duties and powers as shall be designated from time to time by the directors.

Section 5. Resignations and Removals

Any director or officer may resign at any time by delivering his resignation in writing to the president, the treasurer or the clerk or to a meeting of the directors. Such resignation shall be effective upon receipt unless specified to be effective at some other time. A director (including persons elected by directors to fill vacancies in the board) may be removed from office (a) with or without cause by the vote of the holders of a majority of the shares issued and outstanding and entitled to vote in the election of directors, or (b) for cause by vote of a majority of the directors then in office. The directors may remove any officer elected by them with or without cause by the vote of a majority of the directors then in office. A director or officer may be removed for cause only after reasonable notice and opportunity to be heard before the body proposing to remove him. No director or officer resigning, and (except where a right to receive compensation shall be expressly provided in a duly authorized written agreement with the corporation) no director or officer removed, shall have any right to any compensation as such director or officer for any period following his resignation or removal, or any right to damages on account of such removal unless in the case of a resignation, the directors, or in the case of a removal, the body acting on the removal, shall in their or its discretion provide for compensation.

Section 6. Vacancies

Any vacancy in the board of directors, including a vacancy resulting from the enlargement of the board, may be filled by the stockholders or, in the absence of stockholder action, by the directors by vote of a majority of the directors then in office. If the office of the president or the treasurer or the clerk becomes vacant, the directors may elect a successor by vote of a majority of the directors then in office. If the office of any other officer becomes vacant, the directors may elect or appoint a successor by vote of a majority of the directors present. Each such successor shall hold office for the unexpired term, and in the case of the president, the treasurer and the clerk, until his successor is chosen and qualified, or in each case until he sooner dies, resigns, is removed or becomes disqualified. The directors shall have and may exercise all their powers notwithstanding the existence of one or more vacancies in their number.

Section 7. Capital Stock

7.1. *Stock Certificates.* Each stockholder shall be entitled to a certificate stating the number and the class and the designation of the series, if any, of the shares held by him, in such form as shall, in conformity to law, be prescribed from time to time by the directors. Such certificate shall be signed by the president and by the treasurer or an assistant treasurer. In case any officer who has signed shall have ceased to be such officer before such certificate is issued, it may be issued by the corporation with the same effect as if he were such officer at the time of its issue.

7.2. *Loss of Certificates.* In the case of the alleged loss or destruction or the mutilation of certificate of stock, a duplicate certificate may be issued in place thereof, upon such terms as the directors may prescribe.

Section 8. Transfer of Shares of Stock

8.1. *Transfer on Books.* Subject to the restriction, if any, stated or noted on the stock certificate, or in the Articles of Organization, shares of stock may be transferred on the books of the corporation by the surrender to the corporation or its transfer agent of the certificate therefore properly endorsed or accompanied by a written assignment and power of attorney properly executed, with necessary transfer stamps affixed, and with such proof of the authenticity of signature as the directors or the transfer agent of the corporation may reasonably require. Except as may be otherwise required by law, the corporation shall be entitled to treat the record holder of stock as shown on its books as the owner of such stock for all purposes including the payment of dividends and the right to receive notice and to vote with respect thereto, regardless of any transfer, pledge or other dispostion of such stock until the shares have been transferred on the books of the corporation in accordance with the requirements of these by-laws.

It shall be the duty of each stockholder to notify the corporation of his mailing address.

8.2. *Record Date and Closing Transfer Books.* The directors may fix in advance a time, which shall not be more than sixty days before the date of any meeting of stockholders or the date for the payment of any dividend or making of any distribution to stockholders or the last day on which the consent or dissent of stockholder may be effectively expressed for any purpose, as the record date for determining the stockholders having the right to notice of and to vote at such meeting and any adjournment thereof or the right to give such consent or dissent, and in such case only stockholders of record on such record date shall have such right, notwithstanding any transfer of stock on the books of the corporation after the record date; or without fixing such record date the directors may for any of such purposes close the transfer books for all or any part of such period.

Section 9. Indemnification of Directors and Officers

The corporation shall, to the extent legally permissible, indemnify each of its directors and officers (including persons who serve at its request as directors, officers or trustees of another organization in which it has any interest, as a shareholder, creditor or otherwise) against all liabilities and expenses, including amounts paid in satisfaction of judgments, in compromise or as fines and penalties, and counsel fees, reasonably incurred by him in connection with the defense or disposition of any action, suit or other proceeding, whether civil or criminal, in which may be involved or with which he may be threatened, while in office or thereafter, by reason of his being or having been such a director or officer, except with respect to any matter as to which he shall have been adjudicated in any proceeding not to have acted in good faith in the reasonable belief that his action was in the best interests of the corporation; provided, however, that as to any matter disposed of by a compromise payment by such director or officer, pursuant to a consent decree or otherwise, no indemnification either for said payment or for any other expenses shall be provided unless such compromise shall be approved as in the best interests of indemnification: (a)

166

by a disinterested majority of the directors then in office; or (b) by a majority that there has been obtained an opinion in writing of independent legal counsel to the effect that such director or officer appears to have acted in good faith in the reasonable belief that his action was in the best interests of the corporation; or (c) by the holders of a majority of the outstanding stock at the time entitled to vote for directors, voting as a singled class, exclusive of any stock owned by an interested director or officer. The right of indemnification hereby provided shall not be exclusive of or affect any other rights to which any director or officer may be entitled. As used in this Section, the terms "director" and "officer" include their respective heirs, executors and administrators, and an "interested" director or officer is one against whom in such capacity the proceedings in question or another proceeding on the same or similar ground is then pending. Nothing contained in this Section shall affect any rights to indemnification to which corporate personnel other than directors and officers may be entitled by contract or otherwise under law.

Section 10. Corporate Seal

The seal of the corporation will, subject to alteration by the directors, consist of a flat-faced circular die with the word "Massachusetts," together with the name of the corporation and the year of its organization, cut or engraved thereon.

Section 11. Execution of Papers

Except as the directors may generally or in particular cases authorize the execution thereof in some other manner, all deeds, leases, transfers, contracts, bonds, notes, checks, drafts, and other obligations made, accepted, or endorsed by the corporation shall be signed by the president or by the treasurer.

Section 12. Fiscal Year

Except as from time to time otherwise provided by the board of directors, the fiscal year of the corporation shall end on the 31st day of March.

Section 13. Amendments

These by-laws may be altered, amended, or repealed at any annual or special meeting of the stockholders called for the purpose, of which the notice shall specify the subject matter of the proposed alteration, amendment or repeal of the sections to be affected thereby, by vote of the stockholders. These by-laws may also be altered, amended, or repealed by vote of the majority of the directors then in office, except that the directors shall not take any action which provides for indemnification of directors or affects the powers of directors or officers to contract with the corporation, nor any action to amend this Section 13, and except that the directors shall not take any action unless permitted by law.

Any by-law so altered, amended, or repealed by the directors may be further altered or reinstated by the stockholders in the above manner.

Essentials of the Restrictions Placed on the Transfer of Shares of Stock, Articles of Organization

(Note: If you establish a corporation with other stockholders, make sure that when these stockholders wish to dispose of their stock they are required to offer it first to the corporation.)

- Require any individual wishing to sell his stock to notify the directors of the corporation of his desire to do so.
- The potential seller must name an arbitrator.
- Decide how long the directors have to accept the stockholder's offer.
- If the directors cannot accept the offer, or do not wish to do so, they must name a second arbitrator. The two arbitrators will then name a third arbitrator.
- Decide how long the directors have to pay for the stock after a stockholder offer is accepted or an arbitrator judgment as to the stock's value has been rendered.
- Ensure that the administrator of the estate of a deceased stockholder must abide by these procedures.

Sample Restrictive Transfer of Shares of Stock, Articles of Organization

Any stockholder desiring to sell or transfer such stock owned by him shall first offer it to the corporation through the board of directors in the following manner:

- He shall notify the directors of his desire to sell or transfer by notice in writing, which notice shall contain the price at which he is willing to sell or transfer and the name of one arbitrator. The directors will within 30 days thereafter either accept the offer, or by notice to him in writing name a second arbitrator, and these two will name a third. It will then be the duty of the arbitrators to ascertain the book value of the stock, and if any arbitrator shall neglect or refuse to appear at any meeting appointed by the arbitrators, a majority may act in the absence of such arbitrator.

- After the acceptance of the offer, or the report of the arbitrators as to the book value of the stock, the directors shall have 30 days within which to purchase the stock at such valuation, but if at the expiration of 30 days the corporation shall not have exercised the right to so purchase, the owner of the stock shall be at liberty to dispose of the same in any manner he may see fit.

- No shares of stock shall be sold or transferred on the books of the corporation until these provisions have been complied with, but the board of directors may in any particular instance waive the requirement.

- The administrator or executor of the estate of a deceased stockholder shall comply with the terms of this section before attempting to transfer stock to any heirs, assignees, or devisees of the deceased stockholder.

Essentials of the Corporate Purposes Section, Articles of Organization

- Provide a list of the purposes of your corporation, which will ordinarily be required as part of your articles of organization.

- Define your purposes broadly; do not limit your corporation to just one activity.

- Conclude your list of purposes with a general clause allowing you to expand into any business activity permitted by law.

- Add a second list detailing the means you reserve the right to use in realizing your purposes.

Sample Corporate Purposes Section, Articles of Organization

1. The name by which the corporation shall be known is the ABC Corporation.

2. The purposes for which the corporation is formed are:

- To engage in the business of assisting nonprofit organizations in raising funds for their programs and in using funds so raised, including engaging in direct and indirect fund-raising activities, soliciting funding, program development, public relations, and managerial guidance, and such other services generally associated with the financing and use of funding by nonprofit organizations.

- To engage in the presentation, publication, production, and sponsorship of lectures, seminars, courses, workshops, and other such educational or training sessions relating to any and all aspects of fund raising, program development, public relations, and managerial guidance, and to publish or produce books, pamphlets, films, tapes, recordings, and other such materials to be used with or independently of such educational or training sessions.

- To engage in the business of providing teachers, lecturers, and other speakers on any and all subjects to any and all individuals, groups, or organizations who wish such speakers.

- To engage in the business of providing all aspects of managerial and public relations guidance to profit-making businesses, individuals, or corporations.

- To engage in the business of writing, compiling, publishing, and distributing newsletters, newspapers, or other periodicals related to public or private funding opportunities, or to any other subject.

- To engage in the business of providing consultants to profit-making and nonprofit organizations and to individuals.

- To engage in any other business permitted by law.

To perform the above-named business purposes, this corporation will be permitted to use all legal means necessary and proper to the efficient accomplishment of these purposes, including, but not limited to, the following powers:

- To manufacture, purchase, or otherwise acquire goods, merchandise, and property of all kinds, including real property, and to hold, own, mortgage, sell or otherwise dispose of, trade, deal in and with the same.

- To acquire and pay for in cash, stock, or bonds of this corporation, the good will, rights, assets, and property of any person, firm, association, or corporation.

- To apply for, obtain, register, purchase, lease, or otherwise acquire, and to use, own, operate, sell, assign, or otherwise dispose of trademarks, tradenames, copyrights, patents, inventions, improvements, and processes used in connection with or secured under letters patent of the United States or any foreign country.

- To purchase, hold, sell, assign, transfer, mortgage, pledge, or otherwise dispose of shares of the capital stock of,or of any bonds, securities, or evidences of indebtedness created by any other corporation or corporations; and while the owner of such stock, to exercise all the rights, powers, and privileges of ownership, including the right to vote thereon.

- To purchase, hold, reissue, and sell the shares of its own capital stock.

- To enter into, make, perform, and carry out contracts of every kind and for any lawful purpose with any person, firm, association, corporation, or governmental body or agency.

- To borrow or raise money without limit as to amount, and to draw, make, accept, endorse, execute, and issue promissory notes, drafts, bills of exchange, warrants, bonds, debentures, and other negotiable or non-negotiable instruments and evidences of indebtedness, and to secure the payment of any of the foregoing and the interest thereon by mortgage upon or pledge, or assignment in trust of the whole or any part of the property of the corporation, and to sell, pledge, or otherwise dispose of such bonds and other evidences of indebtedness for the purposes of the corporation.

- To conduct business in any of the states, possessions, territories, or dependencies of the United States, in the District of Columbia, and in any and all foreign countries, and to have one or more offices therein without limit as to amount, but always subject to the laws of such state, territory, possession, dependency, or country.

- To recruit, hire, employ and dismiss employees, agents, and independent contractors, without limit as to number of, or amount of payment.

- To have and to exercise all the powers reserved for a corporation organized under and in accordance with the provisions of Chapter 156B of the Massachusetts General Laws, and to do any and all of the things hereinbefore set forth to the same extent as natural persons might and could do, and in any part of the world.

BIBLIOGRAPHY

General Books on Consulting, Organizational Change, and Management

Albert, Kenneth J. **How to be Your Own Management Consultant.**
New York: McGraw Hill, 1978. A management consultant advises executives on how to apply consultants' skills to their own businesses. Provides tips on defining problems, scope, and procedures; quantitative and qualitative analysis; and corporate growth planning.

Productivity Through Consultancy.
Tokyo: Asian Productivity Organization, 1974. One of a series of books on consulting in Asia, particularly in Japan. It features articles on problem analysis, report writing, and management by objective.

Bailey, Geoffrey **Maverick: Succeeding As A Free-Lance Entrepreneur** New York. Franklin Watts, 1982. Includes a chapter on the consulting methods of Dr. Jeffrey Lant.

Blake, Robert R. and Mouton, Jane S. **Consultation.**
Reading, Mass.: Addison Wesley, 1970. A classic on management consulting, organizational development and change.

Blake, Robert R. and Mouton, Jane S. **Diary of an OD Man.**
Houston: Gulf Publishing,1976. An extended case study of an organizational development consultant's involvement in a labor/management dispute.

Burgher, Peter H. **Changement.**
Lexington, Mass. : D.C. Heath, 1979 ($15.95). Twenty-nine articles and chapters on various aspects of managing change.

Clark, Peter A. **Organizational Design, Theory and Practice.**
London: Tavistock, 1972. The application of behavioral science to business and industrial organizational design.

Davey, Neil H. **The External Consultant's Role in Organizational Change.**
Michigan: Michigan State University, 1971. An abundance of often confusing data written in academic jargon.

Fuchs, Jerome H. **Making the Most of Management Consulting Services.**
New York: AMACOM, 1975. General guide on selecting, using, and monitoring consultants. Written for corporate executives. Includes a list of 100 areas of business management consulting.

Goldstein, L. D. **Consulting with Human Service Systems.**
Reading, Mass. : Addison Wesley, 1978. Explores how various models of consultancy theory apply to the special needs of nonprofit human-services organizations.

Gore, George J. and Wright, Robert G. **The Academic Consultant's Connection.**
Dubuque, Iowa: Kendall/Hunt Publishing, 1979. Although directed toward academic readers, this highly recommended book is a useful collection of articles on why consultants are hired, cost/benefit analysis of engagements, defining a service line, client character awareness, and team consulting.

Grossman, Lee. **The Change Agent.**
New York: AMACOM, 1974. Elementary principles on effecting change in business.

Harper, Malcolm. **Consultancy for Small Business.**
Intermediate Technology Publications, 1976. Focuses on meeting the needs of small businesses.

Higdon, Hal. **The Business Healers.**
New York: Random House, 1969. A somewhat dated, general picture of the history and development of large consulting firms.

Hunt, Alfred. **The Management Consultant.**
New York: Basic steps of a consulting engagement, selecting clients/consultants, executive search engagements, staff building and foreign markets.

Kelley, Robert E. **Consulting: The Complete Guide to a Profitable Career**. Recommended for the professional. New York, Charles Sculner & Sons, 1981.

Klein, Howard. **Other People's Business.**
New York: Mason/Charter, 1977. A somewhat prosaic general overview of the history of consultancy primarily from a client's viewpoint. Focuses on consulting's complexities in relation to top management and roles of management consultants.

Kuttner, Monroe S., editor. **University Education for Management Consultants.**
American Institute of CPAs,1979. Explores a university's role in preparing students to become management consultants.

Lippitt, Gordon L. **The Consulting Process in Action.**
La Jolla, Calif. University Associates, 1978.

Naumes, William. **The Entrepreneurial Manager in the Small Business.**
Reading, Mass.: Addison Wesley, 1978. Directed toward managerial consultants who know business administration and who specialize in small business. Articles and case studies on starting a business, financing, strategic planning, entrepreneurship, and economic development.

Shay, Phillip W. "How to Get the Best Results from Management Consultants."
New York: ACME. A 56-page booklet on a client's viewpoint of consultants' roles. Defines problems, measures results.

Wolf, William. **Management and Consulting: An Introduction to James O. McKinsey.**
New York: Cornell University, 1978. Apparently developed from a college thesis, this is an odd, but interesting, review of the career and precepts of the co-founder of Hamilton, McKinsey, one of the largest management-consulting firms.

Bermont, Hubert. **The Successful Consultant's Guide to Authoring, Publishing, and Lecturing.**
Washington, D. C. : Bermont Books, 1979 (120 pages, $25). Covers costs, design, copyrights, production, pricing, and marketing. Like other Bermont books, thin and overpriced.

Bermont, **The Successful Consultant's Guide to Writing Proposals & Reports.**
($10). Includes strategies for consultants, but Gallagher's book (below) is a better guide to developing and writing good reports.

Bjorkman, David. **Write, Publish, and Sell It Yourself.**
Colorado: Hamilton Press (141 pages, $7.95). Available from publisher: 4720 Hancock, Boulder, Colo. 80303. Considered a good guide to the production aspects of self-publishing, but does not cover writing or research.

Coffin, Royce A. **The Negotiator.**
New York: AMACOM, 1973. The American Management Association's basic book on negotiating skills and strategies.

Davidson, Marion and Blue, Martha. **Making it Legal: A Law Primer for the Craftmaker, Visual Artist, and Writer.**
New York: McGraw Hill, 1979. Covers legal and tax aspects for writing and self-publishing.

Ewing, David W. **Writing for Results in Business, Government and the Professions.**
New York: John Wiley and Sons, 1974 (466 pages, hardbound, $18.95). Ewing, the executive editor of the *Harvard Business Review,* covers many precepts and pitfalls of business writing in a chatty, informal style. More comprehensive, but less concise, than Gallagher (below).

Francis, Dave and Young, Don. **Improving Work Groups: A Practical Manual for Team Building.**
San Diego, Calif.: University Associates, 1979 (262 pages, paperbound, $13.50). This is helpful for improving team building and management skills. It provides more practical than theoretical advice.

Gallagher, William J. **Report Writing for Management.**
Reading, Mass.: Addison Wesley, 1969 (215 pages, paperbound, $7.95). Written by the director of communications at Arthur D. Little, Inc., this is one of the best self-help books on report writing.

Hasselstrom, L. M. **The Book Book: A Publishing Handbook.**
South Dakota: Lame Johnny Press, 1979 ($6.95, paperbound, $12.95, cloth). Available from publisher: Box 66, Hermosa, South Dakota 57744. Basic mechanics of producing your own book.

McHugh, John B. **Self-Publishing.**
Ohio: McHugh Associates, 1981 ($12). Available from the publisher; 832 Linworth Road East, Columbus, Ohio 43085. Concentrates solely on financial aspects of self-publishing.

Merry, Uri and Allerhand, Melvin. **Developing Teams and Organizations.**
Reading, Mass.: Addison Wesley, 1977. Behavioral-science-oriented book provides ideas on communicating effectively in groups and varying meeting design to accomplish goals.

Poynter, Dan. **Self-Publishing Manual,** second edition.
Santa Barbara, Calif.: Parachuting Publications, 1980 ($9.95). Available from the publisher: P.O. Box 4232, Santa Barbara, Calif. 93103. A practical guide to self-publishing.

Business Management and Development

Consulting Service: AEA Business Manual No. 151.
Santa Monica, Calif.: American Entrepreneur's Association, 1979. A non-specific and overpriced how-to book on starting a consultancy.

Atman, Mary Ann and Weil, Robert I. **Managing Your Accounting and Consulting Business.**
Matthew Bender, 1978 (640 pages, postbound, $50). Reference book on timekeeping, financial records, equipment, insurance, and assembling a library.

Baumbeck, Clifford M. and Lawyer, Kenneth. **How to Organize and Manage a Small Business,** sixth edition.
New Jersey: Prentice Hall, 1979. A classic textbook with practical and theoretical information on financing, bookkeeping, organization and staffing policy, management, and facilities.

Bermont, Hubert, **How to Become a Successful Consultant in Your Own Field.**
Washington, D.C.: Bermont Books, 1978 (157 pages, hardbound, $20). Available from publisher: 815 15th Street N.W., Washington, D.C. 20005. Bermont's tale of establishing his consultancy is too personal and lacks depth.

Cohn, Theodore and Lindberg, Roy A. **Survival and Growth: Management Strategies for Small Business.**
New York: AMACOM, 1974. Defines the role, problems, and strategies of small businesses.

Dible, Donald M. **Up Your Own Organization.**
Santa Clara, Calif.: The Entrepreneur Press, 1974. Provides sources for venture capital, patents, and business plans and provides a resource bibliography.

Fregley, Bert. **How to Be Self-Employed: Introduction to Small-Business Management.**
Palm Springs, Calif.: Etc. Publications, 1977. Geared primarily toward consulting for small retail shops, with chapters on personnel, profit-and-loss control, accounting, and legal structure.

Frost, Ted S. **Where Have All the Woolly Mammoths Gone: A Small-Business Survival Manual.**
West Nyack, N.Y.: Parker Publishing, 1976. An accountant whose clients are small businesses offer his insights, with chapters on bookkeeping, taxes, and incorporating.

Goodryder, Ernest. **How to Earn Money As a Consultant.**
Business Psychology International (196 pages). Of dubious quality.

Levoy, Robert P. **The $100,000 Practice and How to Build It.**
Englewood Cliffs, N. J.: Prentice Hall, 1966. Provides rather obvious tips to doctors and lawyers on improving client relationships.

Naumes, William. **The Entrepreneurial Manager in the Small Business.**
Reading, Mass.: Addison Wesley, 1978. Provides articles and case studies to managerial consultants who know business administation and who specialize in small businesses. Focuses on starting a business, financing, strategic planning, entrepreneurship and economic development.

Nicholas, Ted. **How to Form Your Own Corporation Without a Lawyer for Under $50.**
14th edition. Delaware: Enterprise Publishing Co., Inc., 1980 ($14.95). Includes the directions and forms needed for incorporating in Delaware. The publisher, a registered agent, uses the book to attract customers. Costs do exceed $50. Including state fees and the agent's minimal services, the bottom line for incorporating is $80, not including legal advice.

Nugent, John W. **The Singleton Markets His Services.**
California: La Cresta Publishers, 1979 (100 pages, $12.75). Available from publisher: P.O. Box 7000-25, Palo Verdes Peninsula, Calif. 90274. Details developing and implementing a marketing plan, reasons to hire consultants, fees and billing, focusing on consulting in training.

Pyeatt, Nancy. **The Consultant's Legal Guide.**
Washington, D.C.: Bermont Books, 1980 (145 pages, $30). Provides information on malpractice, avoiding suits, and estate planning.

Thomsett, Micheal C. **Fundamentals of Bookkeeping and Accounting for the Successful Consultant.**
Washington, D.C.: Bermont Books, 1980 (134 pages, $28). Provides hints on financial planning and management, but is not concrete enough to be a useful how-to book.

Wilson, Aubrey. **The Marketing of Professional Services.**
London, McGraw Hill Ltd., 1972.

Small Business Administration Publications

For order information on these free publications, call 800-368-5855. They will send the complete list of free publications and a list of other helpful publications with their costs. Also, you can check with your local office of the Small Business Administration.

Management Aids

186. Checklist for Developing a Training Program
193. What is the Best Selling Price?
194. Marketing Planning Guidelines
195. Setting Pay for Your Management Jobs
205. Pointers on Using Temporary-Help Services
220. Basic Budgets for Profit Planning
223. Incorporating a Small Business
224. Association Services for Small Business
231. Selecting the Legal Structure for Your Business
233. Planning and Goal Setting for Small Business
236. Tips on Getting More for Your Marketing Dollar
238. Organizing and Staffing a Small Business
239. Techniques of Time Management
245. Exhibiting at Trade Shows
246. Developing New Accounts
248. Can You Make Money with Your Idea or Invention?
249. Should You Lease or Buy Equipment?

Small Marketers Aids

71. Checklist for Going into Business
126. Accounting Services for Small Service Firms
142. Steps in Meeting Your Tax Obligations
144. Getting the Facts for Income Tax Reporting
146. Budgeting in a Small Service Firm
153. Business Plan for Small Service Firms
155. Keeping Records in Small Business
163. Public Relations for Small Business

Small Business Bibliographies

3. Selling by Mail Order
9. Marketing Research Procedures
13. National Directories for Use in Marketing
29. National Mailing List Houses

The following publications, from the **SBA's** small-business management series, are sold by the Superintendent of Documents, Government Printing Office, Washington, D.C. 20402.

Series No.	Title	Stock No.	Pages	Price
15.	Handbook for Small Business Finance	045-000-00139-3	63	$3.00
20.	Ratio Analysis for Small Business	045-000-00150-4	65	$2.20
22.	Practical Business Use of Government Statistics	045-000-00131-8	28	$1.40
30.	Insurance and Risk Management for Small Business	045-000-00037-1	72	$3.00
38.	Management Audit for Small Service Firms	045-000-00131-8	67	$1.80

Selected Free Internal Revenue Service

Publications

Use the numbers on the left when ordering.

Resources: Bibliographies, Listings, and References

(Listed alphabetically by title.)

"Basic Intelligence and Strategic Planning." Daniels, Lorna. 25-page brochure/bibliography available from publisher: Baker Library, Harvard Graduate School of Business Administration, Boston, Mass. 02163 ($3.50).

Consultants and Consulting Organizations Directory. Wasserman, Paul and McClean, Janice, editors. Gale Research Co., Book Tower, Detroit, Mich. 48226.

Dictionary of Business and Management. Wiley-Interscience, New York. 8,000 definitions. ($24.95).

Directory of Management Consultants, second edition, 1980. Available from publisher: Kennedy & Kennedy, Templeton Road, Fitzwilliam, N.H. 03447 (254 pages, $37.50, plus $1 handling charge).

Directory of Management Education Programs. 2,200 programs. Available from publisher: American Management Association, 125 W. 50th St., New York, N.Y. 10020. (1,295 pages in two volumes, $157).

Directory of Personal-Image Consultants. Provides data on consultants who tell you how to speak, dress, and walk for success. Available from publisher: Editorial Services Co., 1140 Avenue of the Americas, New York, N.Y. 10036 (67 pages. $10.95).

Encyclopedia of Professional Management, second edition, 1980. Available from publisher: Kennedy & Kennedy, Templeton Rd., Fitzwilliam, N.H. 03447 (254 pages, $37.50, plus $1 handling charge.)

Findex: Directory of Market Research Reports, Studies and Surveys. Offers a place to check for proposal-writing information. Available from publisher: Information Clearing House, 500 Fifth Ave., New York, N.Y. 10036 ($89.50).

A Guide to Management Services, Dun and Bradstreet, New York, 1968. Describes 92 services from accounting to warehousing that are marketed by consultants and other service providers. Includes references for additional information.

How to Find Information about Companies. Available from publisher: Washington Researchers, 910 17th St., N.W. Washington, D.C. 20006 (284 pages, $45). Identifies sources, such as public records, credit reporting, and trade associations.

How to Win With Information or Lose Without It. Bermont, Hubert and Garvin, Andrew. Available from publisher: Bermont Books, 815 15th St., N.W. Washington, D.C. 20005 ($26). Describes how to find free or inexpensive information on markets, competition, laws, regulations, and technical data. Much of this information is available from the U.S. government, but you must have patience to get it.

Mahon's Industry Guides for Accountants and Auditors. Mahon, James J. Available from publisher: Warren, Gorham and Lamont, 210 South St., Boston, Mass. ($96). Covers 18 industries.

Management Consultant's Bibliography. Available from publisher: Institute of Management Consultants, 19 W. 44th St., New York, N.Y. 10036 (75 pages, $11).

Martindale-Hubbell Law Directory. An annual listing of lawyers admitted to the bar in each state, including advertisements of lawyers' and law firms' specialties.

National Technical Information Services. This division of the U.S. Department of Commerce offers a wide variety of reports and information services based on federally funded research. Subjects include technical information, industry, business, economics, government, health planning, and urban development. Prices from reports are based on cost. NTIS, 5285 Port Royal Rd., Springfield, Va. 22161, telephone 212-724-3509.

Predicasts' F&S Index of Corporations and Industries. Predicasts, Inc., Cleveland, Ohio. Annual directory of periodicals covering acquisitions, mergers, new products, technical developments, government policies, and economic factors. An international version is also available.

The Small Business Index. Kryzak, Wayne D. Scarecrow Press, New Jersey, 1978. Index of books, associations, and periodicals in a diverse list of small service and retail businesses.

Standard & Poor's Register of Corporations, Directors, and Executives. New York: Standard & Poor's Corp. Annual. Lists officers, products, sales, and other information.

Standing Committee on Lawyer Referral Services. This is not a recommended way to find a lawyer, but if you need one, the committee can help. American Bar Association, 1155 E. 60th St., Chicago, Ill. 60637.

University Associates Catalog. U.A., an educational and publishing company, specializes in materials and workshops on management, organizational development, and human-resource development. Includes high-quality offerings by well-known experts. Write U.A., 8517 Production Ave., San Diego, Calif. 92121.

"Wage and Salary Levels." Brochure lists surveys. Available from publisher: Abbott, Langer, and Associates, Box 275, Park Forest, Ill. 60466.

Work Related Abstracts. Information Coordinators, Inc., Detroit, Mich. Annual periodic reference covers human behavior and work, compensation, management science, labor history, education, training, and industrial engineering. It can be found at the library's periodical reference desk.

Writer's Market. Brohaugh, William, editor. Writer's Digest Books, Cincinatti, Ohio. Annual directory of periodical and book publishers. Covers editors, audiences, fees, rights, how to break into the field—everything you need to know for a query letter. (900 pages, hardbound, $14.95; also available in paperback).

Periodicals

Several general-business magazines and newsletters for small business and consulting may be of interest. Subscribe to a general-business periodical to keep abreast of the business community. If you need information about other periodicals, check the **Writer's Market** (see Resources) or **The National Directory of Newsletter and Reporting Services,** published by Gale Research.

Business Week, McGraw Hill Publications, Inc., 1221 Ave. of the Americas, New York, N.Y. 10020. Probably the least sophisticated general-business periodical.

Consultants News, Kennedy & Kennedy, Inc., Templeton Rd., Fitzwilliam, N.H. 03447. ($56 per year). Monthly newsletter covering the major consulting firms, personalities, association conferences, and publications.

Consulting Opportunities Journal, 1629 K St., N.W, Washington, D.C. 20006. Useful for both beginners and experienced consultants.

Dun's Review, Dun & Bradstreet, 666 5th Ave., New York, N.Y. 10019. Emphasizes business management and finances for top executives of large corporations.

Forbes, 60 Fifth Ave., New York, N.Y. 10011. ($30 per year). Biweekly that concentrates on company profiles and general articles.

Fortune, Time, Inc., 541 N. Fairbanks Ct., Chicago, Ill. 60611. ($30 per year). Includes more generic articles than **Forbes**, of moderate sophistication.

Harvard Business Review, Subscription Service Dept., P.O. Box 3000, Woburn, Mass. 01888. ($24 per year). Sophisticated bimonthly journal covering topical and theoretical areas.

Inc., 38 Commercial Wharf, Boston, Mass. 02110. ($18 per year). A small-business monthly magazine with helpful columns on taxes, marketing, law, government, and management strategy.

Sloan Management Review, Sloan School of Management, the Massachusetts Institute of Technology, 50 Memorial Drive, Cambridge, Mass. 02139. ($16 per year). An abstract, theoretical business/management quarterly.

Small Business Management Report, Small Business Monitoring and Research Co., 500 Hartnell St., Monterey, Calif. 93940. ($48 per year). Unavailable for review.

Venture, 35 W. 45th St., New York, N.Y. 10036. Aimed at entrepreneurs.

Wall Street Journal, Subscriptions, 200 Burnett Rd., Chicopee, Mass. 01021. ($77 per year). *The* business daily.

Recent Articles on Consulting

Ad East, November, 1982 "On Consulting" by Dr. Jeffrey Lant. Practical tips for consulting success.

Business Week. May 21, 1979. "The New Shape of Management Consulting." General article on the state of the art, emphasizing specialization.

June 12, 1978. "Consulting Month by Month." Discusses the advantages, for both consultants and clients, of consulting on a monthly basis, rather than a project basis.

Black Enterprise. September, 1979. "So Long Nine-to Five." Lifestyle article on free-lancers and consultants, emphasizing need for discipline, organization, and guts.

California Management Review. Vol. 21, Number 3, Spring, 1979. Article on the management consultant as a problem identifier rather than a problem solver.

Cambridge Express, January 30, 1982 "Mastering the Consulting Game" by Dr. Jeffrey Lant. Ten insightful rules for achieving consulting success.

Dun's Review. March, 1979. "Management Consultants and Conflict of Interest," J.H. Kennedy. Conflicts occur when consultant serves on board of directors and gets involved in recruiting.

November, 1979. "The Accounting Wizards of Wall Street," Arlene Hershman. Profiles of the people who predict and interpret accounting rules for security analysts and investors.

Energy International. Vol 17, No. 9, September, 1980. "Consultants Square up to Government Pressures," Roderick Jones. Describes how engineering consultants compete with the primary purchaser of their services, the U.S. government.

Forbes. May, 25, 1981. "Companies: Intellectics/The Corporate Truth Squad." Profile of a consulting firm that concentrates on eliciting solutions from personnel rather than solving their problems for them.

Harvard Business Review. Number 6, 1979. "Should You Have an Internal Consultant?" R.E. Kelley. Suggests that internal consultants are less expensive and more effective than external consultants and provides advice on making decision between them.

Human Resource Management. No. 2, 1978. "Some Unintended Consequences of Top-Down Organizational Development," B.J. White and V.J. Ramsey. The dangers of imposing an organizational structure without due consideration of organizational character at all hierarchical levels.

Inc. May, 1980. "A Small Company President Talks Back to Consultants." Two specialists in consulting to small businesses, one long-term and the other short-term, argue pros and cons of their services with the president of a small company.

February, 1980. "The Boss Almost Gave Up." Describes how a consultant solved production jams of a small manufacturer.

July, 1979. "Let Outsiders Run Your Business?" Describes how an advisory team of consultants helped a small business that was growing rapidly and needed additional management skills.

Industrial Engineering. June, 1979. "When Do You Hire a Consultant?" W.G. Lyle and D.L. Bates. Describes a methodology for cost/benefit analysis of using consultants.

Journal of Accountancy. Vol. 150, No. 2, August, 1980. "Using Consultants to Meet CPA Needs." Details the pros and cons of using outsiders for continuing professional education in accounting firms.

Journal of Applied Behavioral Science. No. 4, 1977. "Value Dilemmas in Organizational Development," D.D. Bowen. Describes how value dilemmas reduce the effectiveness of organizational development consultants.

No. 4, 1978. "The Effectiveness of Third-Party Process Consultation as a Function of the Consultant's Prestige and Style of Intervention," R. Lipshitz and J.J. Sherwood.

No. 1, 1978. "Stages in Developing a Consulting Relationship: A Case Study of a Long Beginning," R.E. Kaplan. Describes how to prepare an organization to accept change.

Journal of Small Business Management. "Consulting with Small Business: A Process Model," J.C. Bruckman and Steve Iman. Details phases of consulting to small business.

Journal of Systems Management. August, 1979. "Small Business Development Centers," L.L. Byars and C. Christenson. Describes how university-sponsored small business development centers assist entrepreneurs and independents in planning, development, and growth strategies.

Management. June 12, 1978. "Case Study: How a Marketing Consultant Helped a Small Company," D. Joseph.

Management Quarterly. No. 4, 1978-79. "Getting Results from Consultants." Details increased recognition of the need for change, particularly in terms of personal relations.

Management Today. April, 1980. "Two Cheers for Consultancy," Rosemary Brown. Describes how consulting is gaining popularity in England, particularly in personnel and management-information systems.

MBA. No. 6, 1978. "Building Castles in the Bronx," J. Traub. Describes how New York University graduate students run a consulting service to assist in the economic development of a blighted inner-city community.

Money June, 1980. "Bad News Can Be Good News for Management Consultants." Describes management consulting in the 1980's economic environment, emphasizing consulting groups.

Nations Business. February, 1979. "Free Advice Pays Off for Small Business." Details small-business development centers established by the government in cooperation with universities.

New York Times. December 30, 1979, Section IV, page 18. The Bureau of Labor Statistics predicts a decline in the number of self-employed business managers because of their inability to compete with large corporations and chains.

New York Times. November 9, 1979, Section IV, page 7. The Federal Trade Commission is asked to investigate an alleged monopoly by the Big 8 accounting firms.

August 19, 1979, Section III, page 1. D. Ronald Daniel reports on McKinsey and Co.'s decision to stay with traditional consulting style rather than adopt a more technical approach.

June 20, 1979, Section IV, page 13. Elizabeth Fowler reports on the estimated 15 percent annual growth rate of management consulting firms.

June 14, 1979, Section IV, page 1. The first of a series of articles on the battle between the Securities and Exchange Commission and accounting consulting firms on the firms' right to provide non-audit-related services.

Optimum. No. 3, 1978. "What Is A Nice Businessman Like You Doing in a Profession Like This?" R.C. Evans and D.J. Saunders. Canadian management-consulting associations argue about whether the ethics of professional advertising apply to their members.

Personnel Administration. July, 1979. "A Childbirth Model of Organizational Development," S.D. Norton and N. DiMarco. Survey of 250 firms indicates that the most important activity for consultants is to provide the managers of organizational development efforts with insights on their own organizations.

Security Management. September, 1980. "How to Choose and Use Consultants," Mary A. Kmet. Describes why businesses hire consultants and how to avoid common pitfalls that occur in using them.

Training. August, 1979. "Tips for Hiring Your Next Outside Consultant," R.N. Landauer and P.J. Newman. The authors cite references and compatibility as the primary criteria for hiring consultants and suggest requesting a pilot session.

Training & Development. November, 1979. "Use of Management Consultants," S.J. Murdoch. Describes how the expectations and attitudes of the company's executives are as important as the quality of the consultant and offers guidelines.

The Wall Street Journal. April 4, 1981, page 18. Scholars identify the qualities that make entrepreneurs tick.

March 21, 1981, page 34. Details how the GAO claims that government is using consulting firms unnecessarily.

February 14, 1981, page 1. Provides information on how consulting firms are in higher demand as running a business becomes increasingly complicated.

November 25, 1980, page 1. Details how graduates of MBA programs are lured into the consulting field.

September 25, 1980, page 1. Describes how hospitals use consultants.

September 9, 1980, page 33. Describes how small firms use foreign trade consultants to expand outside the U.S.

July 7, 1980, page 6. Shows how Carter tightened up on the government's use of consultants.

October 14, 1979, page 25. Describes fads in consulting.

August 7, 1979, page 1. Details again how MBA graduates are being drawn into the management-consulting field by high salaries.

March 15, 1979, page 19. A debate on accountants providing management-consulting services.

Associations

The following is a selection of consulting and trade associations. If you don't find one that's right for your practice, ask your librarian for *National Trade and professional Associations, a directory edited by Craig Colgate, Washington, D.C.: Columbia Books, Inc. (Annual).*

Names and Addresses	*No. of Members*
American Association of Hospital Consultants 2341 Jefferson Davis Highway Arlington, Va. 22202	130
American Association of Political Consultants Suite 1406, 1101 N. Calvert St. Baltimore, Md. 21202	150
American Consulting Engineers Council Suite 802, 1015 15th St., N.W Washington, D.C. 20005	3,600
American Society of Consulting Planners 1717 N St., N.W. Washington, D.C. 20036	130 firms
Association of Consulting Management Engineers 230 Park Ave. New York, N.Y.	60 firms
Association of Executive Recruiting Consultants 30 Rockfeller Plaza New York, 10020	70 firms
Association of Management Consultants 331 Madison Ave. New York, N.Y. 10017	110
Independent Computer Consultant's Association Box 27412 St. Louis, Mo. 63141	1,200 and 400 firms
Institute of Management Consultants 19 W. 44th St. New York, N.Y. 10036	1,100

National Association of Financial Consultants   180
Suite 302, 2950 S. Jamaica Court
Aurora, Colo. 80014

National Association of Pension Consultants   300
and Administrators   and 200 firms
Suite 300, 3 Piedmont Center
Atlanta, Ga. 30342

National Personnel Consultants   100 firms
Suite 1702, Pennsylvania Building
Philadelphia, Pa. 19102

Project Management Institute   3,000
Box 43
Drexel Hill, Pa. 19026

Public Relations Society of America   9,500
845 Third Ave.
New York, N.Y. 10022

Society of Professional Management Consultants   125
205 W. 89th St.
New York, N.Y. 10024

ABOUT THE AUTHOR

Jeffrey L. Lant is President of Jeffrey Lant Associates, Inc., a management and development firm for nonprofit organizations, based in Cambridge, Massachusetts. He received his B.A. degree *summa cum laude* from the University of California, Santa Barbara; a Certificate of Advanced Graduate Studies in Higher Education Administration from Northeastern University, Boston; and M.A. and Ph.D. degrees from Harvard University, where he was Woodrow Wilson Fellow, Harvard Prize Fellow, and winner of Harvard College's Master's Award. Before forming JLA, Dr. Lant taught and/or administered at Harvard, Boston College and Northeastern University. Dr. Lant is included in *Who's Who In The East, The Dictionary of International Biography, The International Who's Who Of Intellectuals, Men and Women of Distinction, The Book of Honor, Contemporary Authors, Who's Who In Finance and Industry* and other biographical guides. He is also the author of *The Consultant's Kit: Establishing and Operating Your Successful Consulting Business* and *Insubstantial Pageant: Ceremony and Confusion At Queen Victoria's Court.* He is both the Editor of *Our Harvard: Reflections On College Life By Twenty-Two Distinguished Graduates* (Taplinger, 1982) and General Editor of the JLA Nonprofit Technical Assistance Series. In June, 1982 the Governor of Massachusetts awarded him an Official Citation in recognition of his "services to independent business people." He has also been honored by the Boston City Council and the Massachusetts House of Representatives. The Associated Press has called him "one of the top consultants in the country." He is associated with over 20 American colleges and universities through The Mobile University of which he is president.

OTHER JLA PUBLICATIONS, SERVICES AND PRODUCTS

AN INTRODUCTION TO PLANNED GIVING:
FUND RAISING THROUGH BEQUESTS, CHARITABLE REMAINDER TRUSTS, GIFT ANNUITIES AND LIFE INSURANCE

Edited by Daniel W. Vecchitto   Nonprofit Technical Assistance Series
                                                 Volume II

This new book with contributions by eight development experts comes in the nick of time for nonprofit America. Heres's information on:

- Starting a planned giving program
- Bequests
- Charitable remainder unitrusts
- Pooled income funds
- Gift annuities
- Life insurance
- Marketing a planned giving program
- Selling investment objectives to donors

AN INTRODUCTION TO PLANNED GIVING has two purposes: to assist the more than 80% of Americans who die without adequate estate plans, thereby leaving billions of dollars for the probate courts to distribute. These Americans could save taxes, enhance their families' finncial security, and help their favorite charities with a planned gift. This book is also a vital tool enabling nonprofit organizations to find the extra resources they need during an extended period of financial adversity.

AN INTRODUCTION TO PLANNED GIVING offers immediately-usable information on:

- Avoiding unnecessary taxes on income, capital gains and estates
- Charitable gifts that pay donors income for life
- Proven techniques for building productive relationships between donors and charities

"Excellent!" *Grantsmanship Center News*

Excerpted in *Foundation News*

Dr. Jeffrey Lant, "that happy, indominable self-help hormone,"   *Boston Magazine*

Dr. Jeffrey Lant, "the young dean of self-promoters,"   *Boston Globe*

Dr. Jeffrey Lant, "one of the country's top consultants,"   *The Associated Press*

has now written the book you cannot afford to be without if you have a message you want the public to hear, a product or service you want the public to buy . . .

THE UNABASHED SELF-PROMOTER'S GUIDE
WHAT EVERY MAN, WOMAN, CHILD AND ORGANIZATION IN AMERICA NEEDS TO KNOW ABOUT GETTING AHEAD BY EXPLOITING THE MEDIA

Dr. Jeffrey Lant, president of a Cambridge, Massachusetts consulting firm, is now well-established as one of America's most intelligent and provocative self-help, get-ahead authors. His book **Development Today: A Guide For Nonprofit Organizations** is the basic resource text for individuals seeking to raise funds from private citizens, corporations, and foundations. Now in a Revised Second Edition, it has received superlative reviews from trade publications and the nonprofit organizations using it.

Dr. Lant's book **The Consultant's Kit: Establishing and Operating Your Successful Consulting Business** is a national best-seller. Now in a 7th printing, **The Consultant's Kit** was named by *The Boston Globe* as "One of the Best Business Books of 1982." It has been featured in more than 600 radio, television, newspaper and newsletter pieces and has made its author a well-known figure to those entrepreneurs, independent contractors and consultants with a service to sell.

Now there's **THE UNABASHED SELF-PROMOTER'S GUIDE.**

Here is an absolutely unique book. There is nothing like it on the market, nor has there ever been. This is not a standard public relations book, not a standard publicity guide. It is a complete, thorough, intelligent and, humorous look at the gamesmanship of getting ahead by exploiting the media.

Here's what's in it:

- Prerequisites for successful self-promotion: mental and technical
- Crafting a Quintessential American Success Image
- Knowing the available media outlets
- Producing the Standard Media Kit
- Creating and maintaining your Self-Promotion Network
- How the Unabashed Self-Promoter finds and uses information sources
- Producing articles by you: formats you must master
- Arranging articles about you
- Setting up and handling the print media interview
- Piggybacking and Multiple Use
- The Unabashed Self-Promoter in the darkroom: how to use photographs
- Rocking around the clock with the Unabashed Self-Promoter: knowing the electronic media options
- How to arrange your electronic media interview
- Handling your electronic media interview
- Arranging a Media Wave: how to get maximum self-promotional mileage from the media
- Publishing and using books by and about you
- The Self-Promotional possibilities of the Talk Circuit
- When and how to use publicists
- When and how to use negative press
- A Potpourri of promotional possibilities

Like all JLA Publications, **THE UNABASHED SELF-PROMOTER'S GUIDE** also has a Samples section packed with documents, letters, and other pertinent materials ready for use. This section will save you hours of time and creativity.

DEVELOPMENT TODAY: A GUIDE FOR NONPROFIT ORGANIZATIONS

by Dr. Jeffrey Lant

"Jeffrey Lant has fashioned a career of telling charities, worthy causes, and dreamers of the day how to grab big bucks at a time when they are simply not be had."

Boston Globe

If you run a nonprofit organization, serve on the board of a a nonprofit organization, are employed by a nonprofit organization, benefit from a nonprofit organization, or care about the distinctive contributions of nonprofit organizations to American life — this book is for you.

DEVELOPMENT TODAY Is Needed

Reaganomics, shrinking resources, a muddled economy are all threatening both the work and even the existence of America's nonprofit organizations — schools, colleges, hospitals, arts groups, civic betterment societies of every kind. These threatening circumstances have caused many such organizations to go out of business; many more have had to reduce their programs — with as yet incalculable effects on our society. If there was ever a moment in the history of the nonprofit idea for tested, economical fund raising methods, that moment is *now.* DEVELOPMENT TODAY fulfills this pressing need.

DEVELOPMENT TODAY Is Complete

Here, at last, is single book containing all the essential information needed by a nonprofit organization for successful fund raising from individuals, corporations and foundations. In it you'll find practical, useful information on:

- organizing an agency fund raising planning process
- producing inexpensive, compelling fund raising documents
- who to involve in the fund raising process and what they should do
- getting leads to corporate and foundation funding sources
- organizing and coordinating your fund raising effort
- training volunteer solicitors
- ensuring a successful capital fund drive
- arranging popular, lucrative special events
- how to make direct mail work for your organization
- the best way to apply for federal grants

and much, much more.

DEVELOPMENT TODAY Is Unique

DEVELOPMENT TODAY is not theoretical. It is designed to be a working tool for nonprofit organizations needing money. Part of its usefulness is its extensive samples section — over 70 pages of materials which can be put to work right now to help you raise money: successful fund raising documents, letters to funding sources, training materials for volunteer solicitors, pledge cards, log forms, contracts questionnaires, to name only a few — all the pattern documents an agency needs and which are often so difficult to create. No other book on the market offers such an array of practical materials.

DEVELOPMENT TODAY Is Written By A Master

Dr. Jeffrey Lant is well known to nonprofit organizations for his innovative work solving their problems. **DEVELOPMENT TODAY** sets out — in the author's characteristically trenchant style — information gleened from years of effort and experience with dozens of organizations nationwide.

GUIDELINES FOR EFFECTIVE WRITING: QUALITIES AND FORMATS

By Professors Walter Lubars and Albert Sullivan

Without good writing skills, an organization will always have severe problems with its public relations, document development, and all internal communications. Here's the book to help you forestall such unnecessary, expensive problems and enhance all your written communications. Find out through **GUIDELINES FOR EFFECTIVE WRITING** about:

- Crispness: how to eliminate the redundant, banal, diffuse and vague
- Flow: the use of transitions to increase smoothness
- Organization: tips on research, planning, organizing your notes
- Readability: practical rules to keep your reader reading all the way
- Clarity: how to communicate what you really mean
- Color: tips on how to add "style" to your style
- Dynamic punctuation: a new look at how marks move the reader and arouse his interest
- Revising and polishing: eight tips on how to edit and revise your drafts to make them crisp, flowing, properly organized, readable, clear, colorful, vivid and mechanically correct.

JLA WORKSHOPS

For Nonprofit Organizations

Development Training Workshop: This program, originated by Dr. Jeffrey Lant, has been offered in more than 40 cities around the country. Based on **Development Today** and using Dr. Lant's latest research about fund raising, this program deals with raising money from individuals, corporations and foundations. It may be offered either as a one-day intensive program or crafted as a longer or shorter program as needed by your organization. It can also be offered as part of an organization's state, regional or national convention. Discounts are available on texts for programs of over 20 participants. Here's what some participants have said of the program:

"Informal, lively, exciting. . . Dr. Jeffrey Lant will be so sought after it's going to be hard to get into his classes."

> Larry Roberts, President
> Northeastern Christian Junior College
> Villanova, PA

"The Development Training Workshop has got to be one of the best workshops in the field today. I was amazed at the voluminous amount of information and the practicality of it all!"

> Kevin Frederick
> The King's Daughter's School
> Columbia, Tennessee

"Gave me a lot of practical advice . . . addressed the concerns of my organization . . . and with humor!"

> Mary Ann Larkin, Chairperson of Development
> The Watershed Foundation
> Washington, D.C.

Introduction to Planned Giving Workshop: This program is designed to clear up the confusion about a much-misunderstood field and tap new sources of support for hard-pressed organizations. Like the Development Training Workshop, this program can either be a one-day intensive session or may be used in connection with your state, regional or national convention. The following critical topics are covered:

- Why the Economic Recovery Act of 1981 makes planned giving increasingly popular with donors.
- Why it is now more important than ever for charitable organizations to develop viable planning giving programs.
- Making different donor assets work both for the donor and the institution. What to do with real estate, jewelry, art, antiques, as well as cash and securities.
- Charitable bequests: types and tax benefits
- Charitable remainder unitrust and annuity trusts: definitions, examples, and tax implications.
- The planned giving program in a general development effort: how to get it successfully off the ground.

- Specific attention is also given to:

    — pooled income funds
    — charitable lead trusts
    — gifts of life insurance
    — retained life estates

Each workshop participant is given as part of the tuition a copy of JLA's unique publication *An Introduction To Planned Giving* which has been excerpted in both *Foundation News* and the *Journal* of the National Society of Fund Raising Executive.

For Individuals Interested in Part-Time Or Full-Time Consulting

Establishing And Operating Your Successful Consulting Business Workshop: This popular program, already offered in 30 states, provided both established and aspiring consultants the information they need to launch successful part-time or full-time consulting practices. It includes information on:

- determining optimal consulting skills
- selecting a specialty
- getting a first assignment
- how much to charge
- how to avoid giving away free advice
- marketing
- exploiting the media to become *the* recognized expert in your field
- building a Supergroup of independent contractors
- expanding into related fields
- when to subcontract
- noncompetitive agreements
- writing successful proposals
- standardized contracts
- cooperative marketing plans
- setting up an office

In addition to the regular workshop schedule, JLA can book this program into your organization's meetings and conventions as a special feature.

For specific times and places of forthcoming workshops, write JLA for information or call (617) 547-6372.

For Individuals And Organizations Interested in Publicity And Public Relations

The Unabashed Self-Promoter's Workshop is Dr. Jeffrey Lant's newest program. Based on the book of the same name, this workshop is now being offered around the country through The Mobile University, JLA's noncredit continuing education program.

198

This is the course no one can afford to miss who has a message they want America to hear, a product or service they want America to buy. It includes information about:

- prerequisites for promotional success
- fashioning a Quintessential American Success Image
- information sources
- how to create a Standard Media Kit
- the three basic article formats by you
- how to get articles by you published
- arranging and handling the print media interview
- piggybacking and multiple use
- electronic media options
- arranging your media wave
- and much, much more.

Dr. Jeffrey Lant is widely regarded as one of the top workshop and platform speakers in the country as participants in his programs consistently affirm. In this program you can learn the methods which have made him continually sought after by the media.

Products And Services Recommended By Dr. Jeffrey Lant

For Publicity-Seekers

THE PUBLICITY MANUAL by Kate Kelly. One of the best-known volumes in public relations. This is a book you'll want to have in your publicity library.

For Consultants, Independent Service Providers, And Entrepreneurs

THE CONSULTING OPPORTUNITIES JOURNAL. *The* essential publication for consultants and entrepreneurs of every description. Order through JLA and receive — free! — the report on "Marketing Your Consultancy: How To Establish Yourself As The Expert."

For Individuals And Organizations Needing Equipment Of Any Kind

U.S. GOVERNMENT SURPLUS: A COMPLETE BUYER'S MANUAL BY J. Senay. Information on how individuals and organizations can acquire at a fraction of its value government surplus.

For Individuals Interested In Multi-Level Marketing Opportunities

If you are interested in breaking into Multi-Level Marketing, one of the fastest ways to escape the time trap and build a national sales force, JLA maintains a list of recommended companies. If approved, you will work with Dr. Jeffrey Lant in the development of your sales force.

ORDER FORM

1. **THE CONSULTANT'S KIT: ESTABLISHING AND OPERATING YOUR SUCCESSFUL CONSULTING BUSINESS** by Dr. Jeffrey Lant (ISBN 0-940374-07-2) $30.00 . . . . ————

2. **DEVELOPMENT TODAY: A GUIDE FOR NONPROFIT ORGANIZATIONS** by Dr. Jeffrey Lant (ISBN 0-940374-01-3) $24.95 . . . . ————

3. **AN INTRODUCTION TO PLANNED GIVING: FUND RAISING THROUGH BEQUESTS, CHARITABLE REMAINDER TRUSTS, GIFT ANNUITIES, AND LIFE INSURANCE** Edited by Daniel Vecchitto (ISBN 0-940374-02-01) $24.95 . . . . ————

4. **GUIDELINES FOR EFFECTIVE WRITING: QUALITIES AND FORMATS** by Professors Walter Lubars and Albert Sullivan $10.00 . . . . ————

5. **THE UNABASHED SELF-PROMOTER'S GUIDE: WHAT EVERY MAN, WOMAN, CHILD, AND ORGANIZATION IN AMERICA NEEDS TO KNOW ABOUT GETTING AHEAD BY EXPLOITING THE MEDIA** by Dr. Jeffrey Lant (ISBN 0-94034-06-4) $30.00 . . . . ————

6. **PROFESSIONAL'S GUIDE TO PUBLIC RELATIONS SERVICES** by Richard Weiner. 4th edition (ISBN 091-3046-108) $60.00 . . . . ————

7. **PROFESSIONAL'S GUIDE TO PUBLICITY** by Richard Weiner. 3rd edition (ISBN 0-913046-07-8) $9.50 . . . . ————

8. **THE PUBLICITY MANUAL** by Kate Kelly (ISBN 0-9603740-1-9) $29.95 . . . . ————

9. **OXBRIDGE DIRECTORY OF NEWSLETTERS** (ISBN 0-917460-11-1) $60 . . . . ————

10. **U.S. GOVERNMENT SURPLUS: A COMPLETE BUYER'S MANUAL** by J. Senay $7.95 . . . . ————

11. **CONSULTING OPPORTUNITIES JOURNAL** $39.00 one year
$68.00 two years . . . . ————

TOTAL ————

Please make your check payable to JEFFREY LANT ASSOCIATES, INC. When ordering items 1-10 above please add $1.50 postage and handling for any one, $2.50 for any two, and $3 for any three or more. Massachusetts residents add 5% sales tax.

INFORMATION

I would like additional information about the items listed above: (please specify) _____

Please send information about:

1. Publicity services offered by JLA and Dr. Jeffrey Lant   _____

2. JLA Nonprofit Technical Assistance   _____

3. Unabashed Self-Promoter's Workshop   _____

4. Establishing and Operating your Successful Consulting Business Workshop   _____

5. Development Training Workshop   _____

6. Planned Giving Workshop   _____

7. Multi-Level marketing opportunities recommended by JLA   _____

8. I belong to an organization which may be interested in having Dr. Jeffrey Lant as a guest speaker. Please contact me.   _____

Name _____

Address _____

City/Town _____   State _____   Zip _____

Telephone (area code) _____ (number) _____

Jeffrey Lant Associates, Inc.
50 Follen Street, Suite 507
Cambridge, MA 02138
(617) 547-6372